Praise for Sri Chinmoy

"I am so pleased with all the good work you are doing for world peace and for people in so many countries. May we continue to work together and to share together all for the Glory of God and the good of man."

—Mother Teresa
Nobel Peace Laureate

"Your loving heart and profound wisdom are a matter of my boundless admiration."

—Mikhail Gorbachev
Nobel Peace Laureate

"What you are doing is in the interest of the entire humanity and the world."

—Nelson Mandela
President of South Africa and Nobel Peace Laureate

"Thank you very much for all your work."

—Archbishop Desmond Tutu
Nobel Peace Laureate

"From ages past, from the Vedic vision of life, from Lord Buddha, to Christ, to Mahatma Gandhi in our own time, through many saints and savants, the spirit of spirituality in man has been expressed. You personify that spirit in that great tradition. We are deeply indebted to you, and I am personally very grateful to you."

—Laxmi Mall Singvhi
High Commissioner for India to the United Kingdom

"I pray to God that He will bless you and guide you so you may propagate the message of peace."
—Cardinal Basil Hume
Head of the Roman Catholic Church in Great Britain

"Sri Chinmoy will be a great hope of Buddhism to bring the message of Lord Buddha to the people of the world."
—Venerable Pratamkunaporn
Abbot of Wat Po, Royal Temple of Thailand

"The spirit of dedication with which Sri Chinmoy has been devoting his energies in lifting the hearts of men and women into spiritual realms of prayer and meditation for world peace is highly praiseworthy."
—Professor Harmindar Singh
Vice Chairman,
World Conference on Religions and Peace

"Sri Chinmoy is a man of many talents whose life is exemplified by simplicity, humility, self-discipline, compassion, knowledge, understanding, fortitude and complete dedication to the service of God in oneness with humanity."
—Professor Charles Mercieca
Executive Vice President,
International Association of Educators for World Peace

God Is …

God Is ...

Selected Writings of
Sri Chinmoy

Aum Publications • New York

Aum Publications
86-10 Parsons Blvd.
Jamaica, NY 11432

Contents

Introduction

What a piece of work is a man! How noble in
reason! How infinite in faculty! In form and
moving how express and admirable! In action how
like an angel! In apprehension how like a god!
         — WILLIAM SHAKESPEARE

History teaches us that no goal is beyond human
reach. Any goal, no matter how lofty, can and
must surrender to patience, perseverance and
conviction. Such being the case, should the
endeavour to know God be any different?

We scarcely dare imagine it! Yet surely,
amongst the countless billions of human beings
who have passed across life's stage, there have
been a few pilgrim-souls who have in earnest
striven for this Goal of goals and reached its
pinnacle-height.

Sri Chinmoy is one such human being.

From a childhood replete with deep spiritual
experiences, through twenty years of intense
aspiration in a spiritual community, to more than
thirty years of dedicated service to the aspiring

heart of humanity, Sri Chinmoy has devoted his every breath to the realisation and manifestation of that ineffable Reality which we call God.

The proof of the pudding, as Sri Chinmoy himself quotes, is in the eating.

For Mozart, the act of composing was no more than an expression of a reality which he clearly and vividly saw and heard within. Doubtless, were we to ask him for proof of his vision, he would admonish us to listen for the proof in his music.

And so it is with Sri Chinmoy, whose intimate knowledge of God is so lovingly expressed in the selections from his extemporaneous talks, answers to questions and poems collected in this book. If we can but listen to him with an open mind and heart, we shall no doubt be able to share in his vision of the One who lives and breathes in the depths of every human heart.

More importantly, we shall receive boundless inspiration and assurance that, far from being the province of the few, God-realisation is the birthright of all of us.

—The Editors

CHAPTER ONE

God and Humanity

God has a living Breath,
And the name of that Breath is man.
Man has a living Goal,
And the name of that Goal is God.

Man and God are one another's supreme necessity. Man needs God for his highest transcendental realisation and God needs man for His absolute earthly manifestation. Man needs God to realise his highest truth, his highest existence. God needs man to manifest Him here on earth totally, divinely and supremely.

We feel that we need God more than God needs us, but this is wrong. God needs us equally, if not more. Why? He knows our potentialities

and possibilities infinitely better than we do. We
think of ourselves as useless, hopeless, helpless,
but in God's Eye we are really His divine instruments. He wants to use us in infinite ways. This is
His Dream that He wants to transform into Reality. God wants us to be not only infinite but also
eternal and immortal. He knows we have that
capacity because He has given us the capacity.
Now He wants us to utilise our capacity.

*You talk about God, but we do not have any
concept at all of who God is. Who is God?*

God is all Love. God is all Light. God is all
Beauty. God is everything: Truth, Peace, Light,
Bliss in infinite measure. He is with form; He is
without form. If you experience God as Peace,
then you will say God is Peace. If you experience
God as Light, then you will say God is Light. If
you experience God as Love, then you will say
God is Love.

Since we are human beings, according to our
limited understanding we say God is this or God
is that. But God is really everything. If we want to
experience Him as an infinite expanse without
any form, we can do so. Again, if we want to
experience Him intimately as a most illumined
being right in front of us, then He becomes that.

When you touch the God-Tree, you may get the experience of Peace, while somebody else will get the experience of Bliss. So you will say that God is all Peace and he will say that God is all Bliss. But it is the same God, the same Goal. In the process of reaching the Goal we may see it in different ways, but once we really reach it, we can see that it is everything. Then, if we have to describe it, give a definition, we will describe the God-Tree in whichever aspect we like best. We can experience everything, but in our expression, our revelation, we will reveal the aspect we like best.

If God is what you want,
Then He can never come second.
He will always come first.
He will come
As your Confidant.
He will come
As your Advisor supreme.
He will come
As your only Friend.

Is there only one God?

There is one absolute God. But each human being is a portion of God. The Supreme God is like the ocean. Each drop has a little of the consciousness of the ocean; therefore, we can say each drop is a tiny god, a portion of God. If you are a portion of the Infinite, you can say that you also embody the essence of the Infinite.

According to our Indian philosophy, there are as many gods as there are human beings. What do we mean by that? Each human being has God inside him. Most of the time the God inside us is fast asleep. But when we pray and meditate, our God comes forward. The soul, which is God's representative within us, has a complete and inseparable connection with the Absolute God.

God is the divine Gardener.
Inside each flower-soul
He sees
His own new and unique Beauty.

God is your own highest, most illumined, most perfect part. You have two parts: one is higher, one is lower. Most of the time you stay in the lower part. When you become fully aware of your higher part and your lower part is totally transformed and unified with the Highest, at that time you are none other than God. Although it is not yet recognised or revealed, your own highest, most developed, most perfect and illumined part is God. But what you are now is not perfect; it is far from perfection.

> *Man's eternal question is:*
> *Who is God?*
> *God's immediate answer is:*
> *"My child, who else is God,*
> *If not you?"*

Some people claim not to believe in God, but they are still good people and they seem happy. How can you explain this?

No matter which way we appreciate the reality or want to identify ourselves with the reality, we have to feel that we are appreciating and identifying ourselves with Divinity; and this Divinity we call either God or Spirit or Being. If you do not want to call it God, you are at perfect liberty not to do so. But you have to call it happiness. Happiness itself is God. You can appreciate the beauty of nature and if you are happy, then the happiness that you are experiencing is God. In one word, if God has to be defined, then I wish to say God is happiness.

The real reality
Is a simple simplicity
And not a complexity.
Complexity has never been related to reality.

Can God be equivalent to energy?

God is not only equivalent to energy, God Himself is energy. But we have to know what aspect of God appeals to us. If God in the form of energy appeals to us, then God will come to us in the form of infinite energy. But if God in the form of a human being appeals to our mind and heart, He will come and stand right in front of us as a human being in a most luminous form.

When you speak of 'the Supreme', are you referring to God?

Instead of using the word 'God', most of the time I use the word 'Supreme'. I ask my students to do the same, for I feel it gives us a more intimate connection with Him. Although God and the Supreme are one, there is a subtle distinction between the two. When we speak of God-realisation, 'God' is synonymous with the Supreme. But usually when we say 'God', we feel that He embodies a height which is static, like a mountain that is high, but flat. When we use the term 'God', we feel that He has reached His Height and stopped. He does not have a constantly evolving consciousness; He is something finished, a finished product.

But when we say 'Supreme', we know that we are speaking of the Supreme Lord who not only reaches the absolute Highest, but all the time goes beyond, beyond and transcends the Beyond. There is a constant upward movement.

He is eternal and immortal.
He is within this world and beyond it.
He is the Creator,
Both universal and transcendental.

Is it possible to have a philosophical proof of God, or do you have to depend on faith?

You have to depend on your sincerity. If you see something, you can acknowledge it for what it is, or you can call it a mental hallucination. When a spiritual Master is meditating in his highest consciousness, he is offering peace, light and bliss in abundant measure. If you are watching him, immediately you will see the reflection of God-consciousness in him. His consciousness will be changed to such an extent that you are bound to see that he is somewhere else. His face will radiate and you will see something inside him.

Philosophy is in the mind; spirituality is in the heart. If you want to define God with your mind, you will never be able to do it. You have to see God with your heart. The best proof of God is your own consciousness. If you come to a spiritual Master and meditate for a few minutes, you will see the difference in your consciousness. Then let your sincerity be the judge.

> *God does not have to convince you*
> *Of His Existence.*
> *You just convince yourself*
> *That you came into the world*
> *To do something great*
> *And be something good.*

CHAPTER TWO

God's Cosmic Game

God was One, but He wanted to become many. You cannot enjoy a game with only one person. If you want to play any game, you will need more players. God originated Himself out of His own Silence in order to divinely enjoy the Cosmic Game.

If we go deep within, we see that we are only taking a conscious part in God's Cosmic Game. We see that we are not the doers; God is the Doer. We are only His instruments. God is One, but He felt that He wanted to enjoy Himself, to fulfil Himself in millions of shapes and forms. He felt that being One, He was not fully satisfied. Why should He be satisfied with only being the One Infinite? He can also be the multitudinous finite. God is omniscient, omnipotent, omnipresent. If He is omnipotent, then why should He not become like an ant, an infinitely tiny creature?

Because of His omnipotent Power, we think of God as something very great or very vast. But just because God is omniscient and omnipotent, He can also be inside the finite. In this way, God is playing His eternal Game in and through you, through me, through all human beings.

God is infinite, but He houses Himself in each tiny child. Here in the finite, He wants to enjoy Himself and play the tune of the Infinite. Only then does He get the greatest joy. It is in the finite that we are aspiring to achieve the Infinite. Again, the Infinite gets the greatest joy by making itself as tiny as possible.

Finite and infinite: to our outer eyes they seem to be opposites, but in God's Eye they are one. The finite and the Infinite always go together; the one complements the other. The finite wants to reach the absolute Highest, which is the Infinite. The Infinite wants to manifest itself in and through the finite. Then the game is complete. Otherwise it will be only a one-sided game. There will be no joy, no achievement, no fulfilment. In and through the Infinite, the finite is singing its song of realisation. And in and through the finite, the Infinite is singing its song of manifestation.

Lord, I seek and You hide.
I seek because without You
My life-flames do not and cannot burn.
Now Lord, tell me,
Why do You hide?

"Daughter, I hide because
My hiding intensifies your seeking.
It gratifies your loving,
Glorifies your achievement
And immortalises your enlightenment."

What is the purpose of life?

The purpose of life is to manifest the inner divinity. The purpose of life is to become a conscious instrument, a chosen instrument of God. The purpose of life is to manifest the highest Truth which we embody. First we have to see the Truth and feel the Truth. Then we have to reveal and manifest the Truth.

The purpose of life
Is to become one with the Absolute Truth.
This Absolute Truth
Is God the infinite Compassion
And
God the infinite Satisfaction.

The aim of life is to become conscious of the Supreme Reality. The aim of life is to be the conscious expression of the Eternal Being.

Life is evolution. Evolution is the unfoldment from within. Each life is a world in itself. Indeed, each life is a microcosm. Whatever breathes in the vast universe also breathes in each individual life.

The aim of life is to realise God. Realisation can never come to the individual who is inactive. We have to pay the price for it. There is no alternative.

We must love God first if we really love life, for God is not only the Source, but the very Breath of life. Love of God costs nothing, but it is worth much. Our mind knows this truth. Our soul embodies this truth.

I have been loving God unconsciously
For millennia,
But I shall love God consciously
From this moment on.

12

Each person has a soul, and each soul has a nature of its own. The soul, which is the direct representative of God, comes down to earth in order to fulfil the promise that it has made to the Absolute in the highest plane of consciousness, Heaven. Each soul has to manifest its inner divinity here on earth in a specific way. It is through the revelation of its own light that the soul manifests its inner divinity. When the soul, through its own aspiration, realisation, revelation and manifestation, enters into the Cosmic Self, then it completes its journey on earth.

To see the light of your soul, you have to feel that you are not the body, you are not the vital, you are not the mind, you are not the heart, but you are the soul itself. In order to have this experience, you have to feel that you need God and God needs you. You need God to raise your consciousness as high as possible—high, higher, highest. God needs you to manifest Himself in and through you here on earth.

My life is a little boat;
It is a feeble cry.
But my soul is a representative
Of the omnipotent,
Omnipresent and omniscient God.

Can we understand God through just the finite part of His creation?

Let us take God as the vast ocean. You know that the ocean is composed of tiny drops. Millions and billions and trillions of drops make up the ocean. If we know how to identify ourselves both with the vast ocean and with the tiniest drop, then we can see God inside the finite and also in the Infinite. It is on the strength of our oneness with the tiniest drop in the ocean that we can see and feel God. If we can establish our oneness with the finite, then we can see what the Infinite looks like.

If we want to see God in His vast creation, as the creation itself, we can do it. But in the beginning it may be easier to separate Him from His creation and identify ourselves with only a small portion of the entire creation. Even in the small part of God's creation which is right now visible to us, we see infinite variety. What will we do with God's entire creation at this time? Our mind will not be able to grasp it at all. To our limited human mind even the finite earth-reality is infinite. If we can begin to understand this tiny corner of God's vast creation, we can say that we have made considerable inner progress.

It is hard for me to get out of my finite self and feel one with the Infinite.

The finite in us is not aware of the Infinite, but when it is made aware of the Infinite, it has an inferiority complex, and it does not want to be consciously one with the Infinite. Inside the finite is an ignorance-force. But the Infinite feels its oneness with the finite. It feels that there was a time when it was not the entire ocean; it was just a tiny drop, like the finite. Then, from that tiny drop, it widened its consciousness and expanded into the ocean itself. This occurred through the process of evolution.

Again, the Highest, the Absolute Truth, was originally One. God was One, and then He decided to become many. The Infinite consciously decided to become the finite. Knowledge tells us that within the Infinite, we can find the finite; and within the finite, we can find the Infinite. Just because God is infinite, He can enjoy Himself in the tiniest atom as well as in the infinite Vast.

Knowledge tells us something more. Divine knowledge tells us that the many and the One were, from the very beginning, identical; they were made together. The One is the Vision; the many is the Reality. From God's Vision-Power, immediately Reality came into existence. Again, with Reality-Power, Vision came into existence.

God wanted to enjoy Himself. He wanted to offer Nectar, Immortality, to His whole creation. With the creation He felt the expansion of His Self-Form, His manifested Form. When He first created the world, with His inner Vision He saw the ultimate future. Now, slowly, steadily and unerringly, He is unfolding His Vision.

That ancient day
When God created man,
He wanted His blossoming Infinity
To be loved
By His embracing Immortality.

CHAPTER THREE

Seeing God in All

God is constantly taking birth at every moment inside you—in what you say, in what you do and in what you become. God is constantly coming into you in a new form. With each new thought, each new idea, you can feel that a new God has dawned, a new God has taken birth. And what is He doing? He is taking you from lesser knowledge to greater knowledge. At your birth, God was born inside you. God is now at every moment taking birth inside you, making you better, nicer, wiser and more fulfilling. Your best qualities are qualities from God.

Behind my hidden tears
God is preparing Himself
For a new dawn.

Everybody has God inside, but not everybody is able to see God within. One can see God only when one cries for Him. Those who cry for God and pray to God can realise God. Everybody has hunger, but the one who has the money to buy food can eat. Similarly, everybody has God inside, but only he who has an inner cry can see God.

If your whole heart
Cries for God,
Then God's whole Heart
Will come to you.

Why is it that I feel more divinity in a flower than in a piece of wood? Isn't divinity in everything?

Divinity is in everything. God is manifesting in and through me, in and through you, in and through everyone and everything. But in some things or in some individuals we see that this divinity is more fully manifested. What you call darkness has inside it infinitesimal light. In this room you are seeing light, but this light can be immediately increased. There is no end to light. There is effulgent light, boundless light, infinite Light.

In the flower-consciousness God wanted to establish a certain amount of beauty. God did not feel it necessary to make this wall or a piece of wood as beautiful as a flower. But that does not mean that God is unkind to the wood or to the wall. In a play there may be a king and a slave. Also, there may be ordinary subjects. All these different roles are necessary. You cannot have a play with nothing but kings. No, you will need kings, ministers, subjects and so forth in order to have a good play.

In God's creation, also, many different things are necessary. If God wants you to appreciate His Beauty aspect, then He will put a flower, or the stars, or a most beautiful child in front of you. If He wants you to appreciate His Power aspect, then immediately God will bring an elephant or a lion in front of you. If He wants you to appreciate His Vastness, then immediately He will bring the vast sky or sea in front of you. Again, if God wants you to appreciate His infinitesimal, tiniest part, then He will make you think of the atom. So it is up to God what aspect of His He wants you to appreciate. God has all aspects; He has all attributes. But He may decide that He wants you to appreciate one particular aspect of His more than other aspects.

Today God may want you to appreciate His Beauty aspect, tomorrow He may want you to appreciate His Peace aspect, and the day after tomorrow He may want you to appreciate His

19

Power aspect. Whatever aspect you are meant to appreciate, God will put that particular aspect inside your consciousness.

*God's Presence
In my mind-cave,
In my heart-room,
In my life-street
I see, I clearly see!
Therefore, I feel that
My God-realisation-days
Are fast approaching.*

I have found in my search for God that He is all around me and within me. The unity with Him is becoming very understandable. What is puzzling me is the separation. What is the sense of separation?

If you see and feel God around you and within you, then how can you have a sense of separation? Inside me is the heart; inside me is the soul. If something is outside my body, then I can have a feeling of separation. But I cannot separate my heart from my body or from myself because my body and my heart are part and parcel of each other and of my life. If I separate one from the other, then I do not exist at all. If you really feel God within you, then there can be no sense of separation.

What actually happens is that at this moment you are living in your heart and you feel God's Presence within you, but the next moment you are living in the physical mind. At that time you doubt your own existence and you doubt the reality that you have just experienced. When you start doubting, the sense of separativity comes into existence. At that time you feel that you are losing something, that you are separated from something. But you do not lose anything. Once you have got something, it is there within you. But if you do not know how to utilise it all the time at your sweet will, then you feel that you have lost it.

When you pray early in the morning, at that time you feel God's Presence within you and around you. Then, when you enter into the hustle and bustle of life, perhaps you forget God's existence. The moment you forget, you feel a sense of separation. But that sense of separation is not actually caused by the absence of God within you. His Presence is there, but ignorance enters into you and veils your consciousness, which a few hours ago early in the morning helped you identify with God and feel your inseparable oneness with Him.

21

That is why inwardly we try to remain in constant prayer or meditation. Outwardly it is impossible. We have to stay on earth. We have to go to the office; we have to go to school; we have to enter into multifarious activities. But inside our mind, inside our heart, we can do whatever we want. Outwardly we may talk to our friends and do everything that is necessary in our day-to-day life, but inside we can keep the living Presence of God. Since we have the soul within us, we feel we are divine; since we have the aspiring heart within us, we feel we are divine. So also, when we go outside and mix with our friends, we have to remember—not out of pride or vanity, but out of sheer necessity—that we are of the Divine and we are for the Divine.

God's Compassion exists
In every life-experience of yours,
Whether you believe it or not.

We have to feel not only the divinity in ourselves, but also the divinity in others. For in this way we can feel our oneness with the Supreme in mankind. One way to feel our oneness with others is to feel that we are everything. But then we may come to think that we are superior to everyone, and that will only defeat our purpose. If we feel that only we are divine, that only we possess divinity whereas others possess undivine forces, then immediately there will be a clash. But if we feel that we are of the Source, then we shall try also to see the Divine in others. If we feel that we are divine, and while talking and mixing with others, if we can see the Divine in them, then our divinity and their divinity will not quarrel or clash. When we feel that we are divine, it is absolutely true. But at the same time we have to feel that others are also equally divine.

Our difficulty is that most of the time we do not have that kind of feeling. While we are praying at home, we see and feel that God is ours. But the moment we come out of our house and look around at others, we do not try to see God inside them. What we try to see in them is imperfection, something unlike ourselves. After our meditation, we come out of the heart and enter into the mind, or we enter into the vital. Then we try to separate ourselves from others and we see others as undivine. But when we come out into the world, if we can bring with us the divinity we saw and felt during our meditation at home, and if we try to see the same divinity in others, then there is no feeling of separation. And if we see the same thing in others which we feel inside ourselves, then we shall never miss God's Presence. We shall never lose our feeling of oneness with God.

Each time I soulfully pray
And self-givingly meditate,
I see my Lord Supreme blossoming
Beautifully and radiantly
Inside my heart.

What is the cause of this separation between man and God?

The cause of this separation is ignorance. We feel that 'I' and 'my' will give us real joy. It is like a child. If he is very energetic, dynamic or aggressive, he feels satisfaction only when he strikes someone or breaks something. That is his satisfaction; that is his peace. But a grown-up gets joy only by remaining calm, quiet and tranquil. Unfortunately, individuals feel that by maintaining their individuality and personality they can be happy. But that is wrong. Only by entering into universality can we be happy. Individuality and personality will derive satisfaction only from universality. A tiny drop, when it enters into the ocean and loses its individuality and personality, becomes what the infinite ocean is. But before that, if it fights for its own individual existence, what can it do as just a tiny drop? So it is the ignorance in the drop that makes the drop feel that it can be satisfied by maintaining a sense of separativity, which is absurd.

My Lord, is there any time
When You do not love me?
"Yes, My child, there is a time."
When, my Lord, when?
"When you think that you are not
A budding God."

25

What about the fact that we all live in individual homes and do different tasks and things like that? Isn't that separation right there?

Yes, but this is not individuality; it is only the necessity that comes from having respective tasks. With my hand I write, with my mouth I eat, with my eyes I see. Even though they do different things, these are all parts of my body. Each individual also will do what he is supposed to do, but not with a sense of ego. He will do it with a sense of oneness. God has given me the capacity to do a particular thing. He has given you the capacity to do something else. Let us combine our capacities. I will not say that my capacity is superior to yours, and you will not say that your capacity is the only capacity worth having. The difficulty with the world is that everyone feels that he is infinitely more important than everyone else. The problem starts when you stay with your capacities, I stay with mine, and we do not unite our capacities.

CHAPTER FOUR

How to Speak with God

God is everywhere. But if we do not see Him or feel Him inside our hearts, then we will not be able to see Him anywhere. First we have to see Him within us and talk to Him inside our hearts. Then only will we be able to see God and speak to God.

We live in ignorance. That is why we feel that God is somewhere else. But if we go deep within, if we realise the Highest within ourselves, then we will see that our own consciousness is one with God's Consciousness. Right now, an ordinary human being will never dare to say that he and God are one, for he knows that his consciousness is

27

tiny, limited, obstructed. But when the Christ said, "I and my Father are one," he was fully conscious of the fact that his consciousness and God's Consciousness were totally one.

We have to shed soulful tears if we want to embody the Supreme consciously and if we want to fulfil and manifest the Supreme at every moment of our earthly existence. When a child cries, the mother comes running. Similarly, when we cry from the inmost recesses of our heart, our eternal Father, the Supreme, comes running to feed us, to illumine us, to carry us to the Golden Shore of the Beyond.

The Voice of Truth
Will speak to us
Only when our heart becomes
A sacred reservoir.

How can I learn to speak with God?

God is ready to talk with you, but you are not paying attention to Him because you are so fond of hearing the sound of your own voice. If you can start to feel that you have heard the sound of your own voice millions of times, and now you want to hear a much more meaningful and fruitful voice, then you will hear the Voice of God very clearly.

Again, there is a great difference between hearing and listening. You can hear the divine in me now, but you may not listen to it; you may not apply it to your day-to-day activities. If you hear what somebody says, its importance to you may not last even for a second. But if you really listen, then the words are recorded on the tablet of your heart, inside your aspiring being. Then spontaneously that divine message will be manifested in your inner or outer activities. If you want to learn to speak to God, you have to allow God to speak to you. You have to stop talking all the time. Then, when God speaks to you, you have to listen; you have to apply God's divine Message in your day-to-day life.

God is listening.
Just speak quietly.
God is listening.
Just speak devotedly.
Believe me,
God is not and cannot be deaf
To your heart-longing.
His Compassion-Perfection
Has caught the very first faint cry
From your oneness-heart.
God is listening.
Just speak quietly and devotedly.

What do you mean by meditation?

Meditation is the language of God. If we want to know what God's Will is in our life, if we want God to guide us, mould us and fulfil Himself in and through us, then meditation is the language that we must use.

Meditation does not mean just sitting quietly for five or ten minutes. It requires conscious effort. The mind has to be made calm and quiet. At the same time, it has to be vigilant so as not to allow any distracting thoughts or desires to enter. When we can make the mind calm and quiet, we will feel that a new creation is dawning inside us. When the mind is vacant and tranquil and our whole existence becomes an empty vessel, God will fill it with peace, light and bliss.

If you can silence your mind
And ask your heart to speak to God,
Then only are you heading
In the right direction.

When we think that it is we who are trying to meditate, then meditation seems complicated. But real meditation is not done by us. It is done by our Inner Pilot, the Supreme, who is constantly meditating in and through us. We are just the vessel, and we are allowing Him to fill us with His whole Consciousness. We start with our own personal effort, but once we go deep within, we see that it is not our effort that is allowing us to enter into meditation. It is the Supreme who is meditating in and through us with our conscious awareness and consent.

How can one learn meditation?

Each person's soul has its own way of meditating. My way of meditating will not suit you and your way of meditating will not suit me. If you do not have a spiritual Master who can guide you, then you have to go deep within and get your meditation from the inmost recesses of your heart.

If you have a teacher who is a realised soul, his silent gaze will teach you how to meditate. A Master does not have to explain outwardly how to meditate, or give you a specific technique of meditation. He will simply meditate on you and inwardly teach you how to meditate. Your soul will enter into his soul and learn from his soul.

What is the ultimate aim of meditation?

The ultimate aim of meditation is to establish our conscious union with God. We are all God's children, but right now we do not have conscious oneness with God. Someone may believe in God, but this belief is not a reality in his life. He just believes in God because some saint or yogi or spiritual Master has said there is a God or because he has read about God in spiritual books. But if we practise meditation, a day comes when we establish our conscious oneness with God.

> To commune with God,
> Man has his silent meditation.
> To commune with man,
> God has His urgent Peace.

What is the difference between prayer and meditation?

When we pray, we speak and God listens. When we meditate, we listen and God talks. When we pray, we feel that we are going up to God. When we meditate, we try to become calm and quiet and allow peace, light and bliss to descend.

When we pray, often there is a subtle desire for something. We may call it aspiration because we are praying to become good or to have something divine. But there is always a feeling of being a 'divine beggar'. In meditation we do not ask God for anything. We just enter into the sea of His Reality. At that time God gives us more than we could ever imagine.

In prayer we feel that we have nothing and God has everything. In meditation we know that whatever God has, either we also have or we will someday have. We feel that whatever God is, we also are, even though we have not yet brought our divinity forward. When we pray, we ask God for what we want. But when we meditate, God showers on us everything that we need. We see and feel that the whole universe is at our disposal. Heaven and earth do not belong to someone else; they are our own reality.

Since the Supreme is fully aware of all our needs, why is it appropriate to pray?

If you get something through prayer, it only increases its value in your life. You can tell the world, "I prayed for it. That is why I got it." A child is hungry and he tells his mother, "I am hungry." Then the mother feeds the child. Then the child will be able to tell the world, "Look, I have this kind of closeness with my mother." Yes, the mother would have fed the child on her own, but the fact that he asks and his mother listens to his request gives him joy. It means that she is at his beck and call. Because of his inner connection and closeness with his mother, the child can ask the mother to help him.

God sees everything, but if we ask Him for something and He gives it to us, then we get the glory. At that time, however, as individuals we are separated from Him. We feel that God is somewhere and we are somewhere else. We never think that He is inside us. We do not remain in our highest consciousness where we feel that we and God are one. If we feel that we and God are one, then the question of prayer does not arise, for our needs are His needs.

As long as we feel separated from God and feel that we have to ask Him for what we need, then we get joy from our prayer. We feel, "Just because I prayed, God gave me what I wanted, so I am worthy of having His Compassion." He would have done it unconditionally, but we would not have had the same kind of satisfaction.

In a race, if somebody tries very hard and runs the whole course, she will be so delighted when I give her a trophy. She has run with such difficulty and with so much trouble, and she feels that she has earned the trophy. Now, even if you do not finish the race, I can also give you a trophy, because the trophy is there, but you will not feel satisfied because you have done nothing. God can give everything unconditionally, but you will not be happy, whereas the person who tries and shows the capacity really deserves what he gets. Here the fulfilment of our prayer is the trophy. If

somebody prays and meditates and gets something, he will get more satisfaction than if God
had given him the thing unconditionally.

Prayer intensifies our intimacy with the Supreme. Meditation increases our oneness with the
Supreme. Before we meditate, if we pray for a few
seconds, then we are developing our intimate
connection with the Supreme. Then, once we
start meditating, we are developing our oneness-
reality with the Supreme. Unless we are intimate,
how can we become one? First we have to feel
that we and God are intimate friends; then we
can realise our oneness-reality with God.

God hears
The soulful prayers of a seeker
Not only with great readiness
But also with immediate oneness.

**Can we answer our own questions through our
daily meditation?**

Any question you have can be answered during
your meditation or at the end of your meditation.
If you go deep within, you are bound to get an
answer. But when you get an answer, please try to

determine whether it is coming from the soul, the heart or the mind. If it comes from the heart or the soul, then you will get a sense of relief, a sense of peace. You will see that no contradictory thought is following the answer. But if the answer does not come from the heart or the soul, then the mind will come to the fore and contradict the idea you have received.

God answers my prayers
Only when He sees
That I shall not misuse
His Answer.

What is the most important thing for the spiritual seeker to remember?

The spiritual seeker should always bear in mind that he is of God and he is for God. Right now he may be a budding seeker, he may be a beginner; so for him God cannot be or need not be always a living reality. Sometimes the aspirant will only be able to imagine God. Sometimes, in spite of his outer efforts, he may not feel the Presence of God in himself, and sometimes he may even forget the existence of God.

But he has to bear in mind that he has a Source and that Source is Light, boundless Light, infinite Light. He has been wallowing in the pleasures of ignorance for many years. But he has to feel that his Source is not ignorance; his Source is Light and Delight. He is for that Source and he is making a conscious effort to return to his Source. While returning, he is manifesting God-Delight here on earth. Even now he is in ignorance to some degree, but he is always for God-Life and he is always for God-Light. If he can remember this, then he will feel a constant sense of satisfaction in his life. He will feel Light, more Light, abundant Light, infinite Light in his outer and inner life.

How can we increase our need for God?

It is very easy. Start by minimising your personal needs. The more you can minimise your personal needs, the sooner you will increase your need for God. If you have ten desires, then reduce the number to nine or eight. Then, some time later, bring it to seven desires. Immediately you will see that just because you have decreased your desires, your love for God and your need for God are increasing.

Again, sometimes we make ourselves feel that we do not need anything from the world but the world needs us. That kind of feeling is equally bad. If we try to fulfil the needs of the world, we will find that it is simply impossible. Today the world will have one need; tomorrow it will have another need. There will be an endless series of needs.

The world does not need us and we do not need the world as such, but we do need the Supreme in the world. You do need the Supreme in your father, in your mother, in your relatives and in humanity. But if you feel that you need human beings as such, then it is simply absurd. You are not going to get anything that you need from humanity.

To come back to your question, your need for God will increase immediately when your need to fulfil your desires decreases. Each time you can discard a desire, you will see that your love-power and your need for God will increase.

CHAPTER FIVE

A Personal Approach to God

Each person has his own conception of God. If the conception of God as Light satisfies you, then you are perfectly right in thinking of God as Light. Someone else perhaps will be satisfied only with God as a most luminous being, like a most beautiful child. Each person has to think of God according to his own inner capacity and inner receptivity.

If you want to see God in a particular form, if you have pleased Him, then He is bound to appear before you in that form. If you want to see Him with attributes, if you have pleased Him, He will show Himself to you with attributes. If you want to see Him in His impersonal Form, as infinite Peace, Light and Bliss, then He can appear in that way also. God is more than ready to appear before you in the form to which you are most devoted.

The personal God and impersonal God are both the same God. The personal God will come to you with a body. He will be most luminous, infinitely more beautiful than the most beautiful human being on earth. The impersonal aspect of God is His infinite Energy, infinite Light, infinite Power. When a man stands in front of you, he is personal. But the moment he shows you his power or his capacity in any form, that aspect is impersonal. Similarly, God is both personal and impersonal; He is with form and He is without form. At the same time, God transcends both form and formlessness.

Personal and impersonal,
With form and without,
God the Supreme
Encompasses all.

Do not try to approach God with your thinking mind. It may only stimulate your intellectual ideas.

Try to approach God with your crying heart. It will awaken your soulful, spiritual consciousness.

Is it better for us to think of God in personal terms or in impersonal terms?

It is easier to approach God in His personal aspect. If we try from the very beginning to enter into the impersonal God, our physical mind—which is so clever—may try to convince us that God is unreal, or we may enter into false imagination. Imagination is not bad, but it can be all mental fantasies. But if we see a most luminous being right in front of us, and then if we try to enter into the heart of this being, there we will also see the formless. If we go from the form to the formless, the process is easier.

Suppose we see someone standing in front of us. If we know that this person is our father, then we can try to see how much knowledge, wisdom and capacity he has. But if we first try to fathom his knowledge without thinking of the person as our father, then we will be totally lost. If we know that he is our father, immediately his affection and love enter into us and then we can easily see his capacity. At that time, it is impossible for us to separate his capacity from his reality.

A commander has a big battalion and inside him is the power to make this battalion do something. He may say just one or two words and then, with the power that he wields, he leaves the whole world stunned. He utters one word of command and immediately his power is seen all over. Once we see him and his capacity, it is impossible to separate his capacity from his reality. It is the same with the personal God. Once we see Him and realise where this immense capacity is coming from, then it is impossible to separate the Being and the capacity.

First let us take the form as reality and from the form let us go to the formless reality. To go to the formless reality from the form is infinitely easier than the other way around.

It seems to me that at the start of the spiritual path we see God with form, and that as we grow into oneness He starts to lose His Form. Is this true?

No, unfortunately you are mistaken. It is our own mental conception that the formless is something superior to the form. We feel that before the creation the Supreme was formless and only later He took a form to come to us. But look at the sun. Although it is so vast, when we look at it, it has the form of a tiny disk. Why? Because we are seeing it from very, very far away.

Similarly, when spiritual Masters, great spiritual figures or God-realised souls come down, they embody the highest infinite Consciousness inside them. But when they come into the world of form, they are 6' or 5'8" or even of shorter stature. Do you think they have then lost their inner height? Do you think they have lost their inner depth? No. It is like the vast sun that looks tiny here.

When consciousness descends into the physical, the physical takes a form. The individual is actually the soul, and the soul is the representative of God. The soul is infinite Peace, Light and Bliss inside God. But we do not see the soul; we see only the very limited frame of the body: this much height, this much length, this much breadth. We feel that something beyond the body or form is vaster. True, it is vaster, but it is a mistake if we say that the formless is more meaningful than the form.

The idea that the higher we go, the more we are in touch with the formless is not true. When we go higher it need not be toward the formless. It can be toward the supremely divine God with form, who possesses boundless Affection, boundless Love, boundless Concern—everything in infinite measure. We can go beyond the form of the mind, but not beyond the supreme Form.

The formless is not superior to the form. They are equally important. Especially in the beginning, before you realise God, it is advisable to go through the form. If you can go through the form to the formless, then you will be happy. But if you try to go through the formless to the form, you will find it impossible. First you have to enter into the water and swim a little. Then when you become a great swimmer, you can cross the sea. But if you try to cross the sea without knowing how to swim, you will drown.

Do you think that one's visions of God as form are influenced by one's cultural upbringing?

Sometimes one may have a vision of God that is influenced by one's tradition or culture. But again, it may not be so. When, on the strength of our own aspiration, we realise God, it is up to God how He will appear before us. In some countries they have very fixed ideas, fixed notions that God will be like this or like that. The Indian gods and goddesses have all kinds of forms. Again, there are many Westerners who have not read Indian books at all, but they get experiences of the Indian cosmic gods and goddesses.

At the same time, there are many Indians who have not studied the Bible or the Western scriptures, but they do see angels and other things. If religious tradition has formed some mental concept of God, the seekers may see God in this way when they are realising the Truth. In other cases, what they see may be entirely determined by God's own Will operating in and through them.

When you speak of the Beloved Supreme Himself, how do you imagine the Supreme to be?

It is not a matter of imagination; it is a matter of experience. You can experience the Beloved Supreme in one particular way. I may experience Him in a different way. Each one, on the strength of his or her aspiration, experience and realisation, will see the Supreme in a different but most convincing way.

If I am looking for a policeman and I find someone in a policeman's uniform, I will be very pleased. Because he is wearing his uniform, I will know that he is a policeman. But if you are looking for a policeman, and you happen to know that so-and-so is a policeman, then you will be in a position to approach him even if he is not wearing his uniform. Similarly, if one is already in tune with the higher realities, he will have the experience of the Beloved Supreme in one form, whereas someone who is having the experience of the Highest for the first time may have it in a different way.

It is like the child whose father is a Supreme Court judge. When the child sees his father in ordinary street clothes, he still knows that his father is a Supreme Court judge. And when he goes to the courtroom and sees his father in a judge's robe, he still knows that this individual is his father.

45

But if somebody who is not a member of the family sees the judge on the street, he will not recognise him. Similarly, each individual sees the Beloved Supreme in a specific way that will be totally convincing to him.

What has been your experience of God?

I have experienced God in the personal form as well as the impersonal form. At this moment, I see Him as an expanse of Light and Delight. The next moment He may take the form of a most luminous being. When we realise the Highest, we see that He is at once personal and impersonal. Like water and ice, He can be with form or without. Sometimes water is liquid, and we can swim in it. Other times it is solid, and we can walk on it. In the spiritual life also, sometimes we are fond of the impersonal aspect of the Highest Absolute, and sometimes we are fond of the personal aspect.

The Highest is beyond personal and impersonal but, at the same time, He embodies both. The Highest is formless, and at the same time He is with form. If we have to state in a word what He is, we have to say that He is both, and again, that He is beyond both. We cannot grasp God with the human mind. In the beginning He is this; then He is that. Then there comes a time when He is beyond both. The Highest is the ever-transcending Reality. Today's Beyond is tomorrow's starting point.

How does the Supreme appear to you, and what is the nature of your relationship to Him?

Usually I see the Supreme in the form of a golden Being, a most illumined and illumining Being. Here on earth, when we say that a child is extremely beautiful, we are judging his form. But the Supreme is infinitely more beautiful than any human child we can see. This is the way I see the Supreme when I converse with Him. It is this form that I am most fond of.

Our relationship is that of Father and son. Out of His infinite Compassion, He has kindled the flames of aspiration in me. These flames climb high, higher, highest. My aspiration carries unconditional love, devotion and surrender.

Familiarity breeds contempt in the human life, but in the spiritual life the familiarity between the seeker and the Supreme Pilot only increases in intensity and capacity. Familiarity cannot diminish the sweetness, love and concern that flows between the seeker and the Supreme. On the contrary, familiarity only increases these qualities. When I deal with the personal aspect of the

Supreme, He increases my love, devotion and surrender. He makes me aware of what He eternally is. The more familiar we become with Him, the more we establish our ever-fulfilling oneness with Him.

The personal aspect cannot create problems for the true seeker. When two people become close, it often does not last because they see weaknesses in each other. But the personal aspect of the Supreme knows what we are. He does not think of us as imperfect; he takes us as His own infinite extensions. He does not find fault with us either on the physical plane or on the psychic plane. It is He that is carrying us to the ever-transcending Perfection.

God always treats you
As His dearest child.
But where is your heart
To feel it,
And where is your mind
To believe it?

Every day when you meditate, try to feel that you are inside the Heart of God, the Inner Pilot. Although you have not seen the Supreme, just imagine a being who is absolutely golden. Imagine that He is right in front of you or that you are inside His Heart or in His Lap or at His Feet. Do not think that you are eighteen or forty or sixty years old. No! Think that you are only one month old and that you are inside the very Heart of the Supreme or in His Lap.

Each moment is an opportunity
To think of God
And to feel God's Presence.
In everything that you do,
Feel that you are touching
The very Breath
Of your Beloved Supreme.

*I completely forgot
That God is old.
I could have learned
So much from Him.*

*I completely forgot
That God is young.
I should have invited Him
To come into my heart-garden
And play with me.*

CHAPTER SIX

God the Father,
God the Mother,
God the Friend

*Aspiration tells me that my God is
Compassion-Mother.
Realisation tells me that my God is
Liberation-Father.
God-oneness tells me that my God is
Perfection-Friend.*

God is at once our Divine Father and our Divine
Mother. In the West, God the Father is promi-
nent, while in the East, in India especially, God
the Mother comes first. Both East and West are
perfectly right. When we realise God the Father,
we are bound to see God the Mother within

Him. When we realise God the Mother, we will unmistakably see God the Father within Her.

When we approach God the Father, we feel His Wisdom, His inner Light, His Vastness. When we approach God the Mother, we feel infinite Love, infinite Compassion, infinite Concern. It is not that God the Father does not have Compassion. He also has it. But God expresses Love, Compassion and Concern through the feminine form more than through the masculine form. In the masculine form He offers Wisdom, Light, Vastness.

Each of these divine qualities—Love, Compassion, Concern, Vastness, Light and Wisdom—is of paramount importance in the life of each aspiring soul. When we feel in the inmost recesses of our heart God's Love, Concern and Compassion and His Wisdom, Light and Vastness, we know that today's unfulfilled man will soon turn into tomorrow's realised, fulfilled and manifested God.

When a human mother notices the shortcomings, imperfections and weaknesses of her child, what does she do? She hides them carefully and secretly. She will never even think of exposing her own child to the world.

Similarly, the Divine Mother, who is infinitely more loving and compassionate than any human mother, can never expose Her child. Like the human mother, She hides the teeming imperfections of Her child from others; then She makes Her child aware of his shortcomings because She does not want him to repeat the same mistake. If he repeats the same mistake again and again, God-realisation will always remain a far cry for him. When She makes him aware of his mistakes, of his ignorance, She does it with the best intentions in order that he may know the difference between an ignorant life and a life of wisdom. The Mother Divine does not delay. She carries the child one step forward. She transforms the child's ignorance into wisdom-light. She transforms his weakness into strength. She transforms his life of night into a life of light.

I often hear you refer to God as 'He'. I see God as all spirit.

A child calls his father 'Daddy'. The father's friends call him by another name, and his relatives may call him by a different name. Those at the office may call him by yet another name. Nonetheless he is the same man. Similarly, each aspirant can have his own name by which he calls God. It is a matter of personal preference.

In my case, by referring to God as 'He', I am not denying that God is also the Divine Mother, far from it. God is the Mother. God is the Father.

God is Light. God is Peace. God is infinite Energy. When I refer to God as 'He', I am not taking anything away from God. God will come with all that He is, no matter whether I call Him Father, Mother or Brahma. God does not mind which name we use as long as our call is sincere. Then He simply comes to answer His child's call.

Your Lord Supreme
Is not standing in front of you
With an iron rod
Ready to strike you
The moment you make any mistake.
Far from it!
Through your obedience-light
One day you will realise
His Oneness-Delight with you.

Is it better to see God as Mother or Father?

On the one hand, just as the soul is neither masculine nor feminine, neither is God masculine nor feminine. Masculine and feminine are only seen in the mind. At the highest level there is only God. Again, a seeker can see God and speak to God the way he wants to. If he cares for the qualities of the Mother, then he will approach God the Mother. But Mother and Father are always one.

When we approach God the Mother, it is like the human mother. The human mother always feels her son is a child, even if he is sixty years old. The mother will always show overwhelming affection, love, concern and compassion. The mother will try to give the child everything all at once.

The father also has boundless love, concern and blessings, but he is more practical; he will not spoil the child. The father feels the child may squander their wealth. Only when the child is more mature, more advanced, will he give him money. But the mother feels, "No, just because he is my child, let me give him all our wealth. Even if he misuses it, no harm. We have plenty."

It is always easier and faster if one can approach God the Mother. When the child cries, immediately the mother comes. But the realisation is the same whether one approaches God the Mother or God the Father.

God the Father
Is all protection to the seeker.
God the Mother
Is all nourishment to the seeker.

Can God also be seen as a child?

If we feel that God is a very old man, like a grand-father or great-grandfather, all the time pointing out our mistakes and errors, then we are mistaken. We must feel that the omniscient, omnipotent, omnipresent God is our real eternal Friend and Comrade. We must feel that we are all children and that He is our age. In terms of our realisation we are all beginners, because our goal is infinite Light and infinite Bliss, and we have yet to come near the threshold.

> *There is a child*
> *Crying for you*
> *Inside your heart-life.*
> *Do you know its name?*
> *Soul.*
>
> *There is a child*
> *Waiting for you*
> *Inside your soul-love.*
> *Do you know its name?*
> *God.*

If we are sincere with ourselves and feel that we are all beginners, all children, then we can feel that God is coming to us as a Child because His Purpose is to play with us. Grown-ups will not play, but a child constantly wants to play, all the time and everywhere. If we feel the necessity of always remaining children, then God can come to us in the form of a Child. He is the eternal Player in His eternal Garden; today He plays with our desires, tomorrow He will play with our aspiration, and the day after tomorrow He will play with our realisation.

When we are consciously praying, concentrating and meditating, God peeps at us like a child. He sees whether we are actually meditating or not. It is like a child peeping through the window to see what his parents or older people are doing. When the child sees he is going to be caught, he runs away.

God the divine Child wants to play His Cosmic Game of hide-and-seek with us. When God hides, we have to seek Him; when we hide, God will come and seek us. In that way we become the sweetest of friends, eternal friends. If God is one-pointed, if He is always catching us with His Knowledge, Wisdom and Vision, then there will be no Game. If one party in a game is by far stronger than the other party and always wins, then the loser will not continue playing. So God comes in the form of a child and peeps at us, His children.

> God is my constant Playmate.
> *Therefore*
> My heart is sailing directly
> Towards His Silence-Home.

What is the most effective way to think of the Supreme as my friend?

Sometimes you inwardly talk to yourself or you talk to a friend. Your friend may be hundreds of miles away from you. Physically you cannot see him, but you can feel his vibration. In the same way, try to imagine that there is an eternal Friend inside you, and that is the Supreme.

When you are speaking to your friend mentally, he may not be able to hear you. But when you talk to the Supreme, He is definitely listening to you. When you can feel that there is somebody listening to you, when you can feel His Presence, then automatically your way of talking to the Supreme will be complete.

If your consciousness
Remains deep inside your heart
And you are constantly
Thinking of God,
Then all your problems will be solved,
Even if you simply ignore them.
Needless to say,
This applies only to you,
Since you are a soulfully sincere seeker.

When I have problems I can't seem to really solve them. Even my friends and parents don't always know what is best. Will it help if I think of the Supreme as my friend and ask the Supreme how to solve them?

There is somebody who knows what is best for us and that person is the Supreme. The Supreme is not a mental hallucination. We will be able to see Him, we will be able to speak to Him, we will be able to dine with Him. He is not only our Father; He is also our eternal Comrade. We have to give Him responsibility for us. Each time we are attacked by a problem, instead of trying to solve it ourselves, with our limited capacity or wisdom, we have to offer it to the Supreme.

59

His Eyes have better vision than ours. His Ears hear more quickly than our human ears. We talk to human beings who have no time to hear us; they have so many things to do in the outer world. But we very often forget that there is somebody else who is always eager to hear from us, even though we do not speak to Him. Sometimes we speak to our own mind, to our own dissatisfied vital, but rarely do we try to speak to our inner being. If we discover the secret of speaking to our inner being, then we will solve all our problems.

If you are loyal to God
And take Him as your only Friend,
How can you have any serious problems?
Impossible!
Even your mind-problems
Will be taken care of
By His Heart's Compassion-Concern-Sky.

CHAPTER SEVEN

God-Realisation

No mind, no form, I only exist;
Now ceased all will and thought.
The final end of Nature's dance:
I am It whom I have sought.

A realm of Bliss bare, ultimate,
Beyond both knower and known,
A rest immense I enjoy at last;
I face the One alone.

I have crossed the secret ways of life;
I have become the Goal.
The Truth immutable is revealed:
I am the way, the God-Soul.

My spirit aware of all the heights,
I am mute in the core of the Sun.
I barter nothing with time and deeds;
My cosmic play is done.

God can be seen. He can be felt. He can be realised. When He is seen, He is Existence. When He is felt, He is Consciousness. When He is realised, He is Delight. In His embodiment of Existence, He is eternal. In His revelation of Consciousness, He is infinite. In His manifestation of Delight, He is immortal. His Vision Transcendental and His Reality Absolute are man's future achievements. Man's expanding love, crying devotion and glowing surrender are God's future possessions.

The world tells you a frightening secret:
God is austere;
God is demanding;
God is stern.
I tell you an illumining secret:
God is reachable;
God is lovable;
God is enjoyable.
When your mind is calm, God is reachable.
When your heart is pure, God is lovable.
When your soul is sure, God is enjoyable.

For God-realisation, the first and foremost necessity is peace of mind. How can we have peace of mind? There are a few ways. If we decrease our earthly needs and increase our Heavenly needs, then we can get peace of mind. Also, if we do not expect anything from anyone or from anything except from God, then we can have peace of mind. As long as there is expectation, human expectation or earthly expectation, we cannot have peace of mind. Again, we cannot have peace of mind by positive or negative renunciation, but by affirmative acceptance. We have to accept the real Reality of God that is inside the world. Then, with our inner cry, with our aspiration, we have to create receptivity inside our body-consciousness so that we can welcome God the Supreme Beloved with His boundless Light and Delight.

In order for us to realise God, we also need purity, especially in our emotional vital. When we purify our emotional vital, we see and feel God's Presence. Then we have to establish clarity in the mind. When we establish clarity in the mind, we will be able to see God very intimately. Then we have to commune with God all the time. In order to commune with God all the time, we have to create the supreme necessity for this inside our heart. This necessity has to be our psychic necessity. When we have created a psychic necessity to commune with God all the time, we shall without fail see God, talk to God, grow into the very image of God and consciously participate in God's Cosmic Drama as devoted and unconditional instruments of God.

Wherever we are, God is. In order to realise this supreme truth, we have to return what we have borrowed from the world: darkness, ignorance, bondage, limitation, imperfection and death. We borrowed these things because we felt that they would help us considerably, but now we have come to realise that they are real obstructions. So these things we must return, and the things that we eternally have in the inmost recesses of our being—peace, light, bliss, truth—we have to increase. We have to bring them to the fore, for they are the real Reality of our existence. The things that we eternally are, we have to claim and offer to the world at large. If we do this, we shall know who God is and where God is.

The moment you know
Who you really are,
All secrets of the world
Will be an open book to you.

What exactly do you mean by God-realisation?

God-realisation means self-discovery in the highest sense of the term—the conscious realisation of your oneness with God. As long as you remain in ignorance, you will feel that God is somebody else, who has infinite Power, whereas you are the feeblest person on earth. But the moment you realise God, you come to know that you and God are absolutely one in both the inner and the outer life. God-realisation means your identification with your own absolutely highest Self.

You may have studied books on God and people may have told you that God is in everybody. But until you have realised God, this is all mental speculation. When you are God-realised, you consciously know what God is, what He looks like, what He wills. You remain in God's Consciousness and speak to God face to face. You see God both in the finite and in the Infinite; you see God as both personal and impersonal.

This is not mental hallucination or imagination; it is all direct reality. When one speaks to a human being, there is always a veil of ignorance, darkness, imperfection and misunderstanding. But between God and the inner being of one who has realised Him, there can be no ignorance, no veil. You can speak to God more clearly, more intimately, more openly than to a human being.

Is it the soul that realises God?

The soul is a portion of God and it is eternally for God. It is our body, vital, mind and heart that have not realised God. The soul knows who God is and where God is and what God is; but the human being only gets glimpses. The human being must practise spirituality and inner discipline and realise the Highest.

When the human in us realises the Highest, at that time there is no difference between us and God. At that time the body, vital and mind become inseparably one and they embody, reveal and manifest the Highest. There is no difference between that illumined consciousness and the highest Reality itself.

It is the human in us that realises God, not the soul. The soul has to manifest God to the world at large; that is why the soul has come into the world.

There are only
Three special lessons
That you have to study
For your God-realisation:
Love God soulfully,
Devote yourself to God sleeplessly
And surrender to God's Will
Willingly, cheerfully and breathlessly.

What is the difference between seeing God and realising God?

There is a great difference between seeing God and realising God. When we see God, we can see Him as an individual or as an object or as something else. But we may not consciously and continuously embody Him and feel that He is our very own. What we do not embody, we cannot reveal or manifest. But when we realise God, we become one with God's Consciousness and God becomes part and parcel of our life.

If we see something, the vision may last for a short while; but when we realise something, this knowledge lasts forever. There is a great difference between experience and realisation. Experience is something that lasts for a few hours or a few days or years; it does not last forever. Experience enters into our life but it does not and cannot make its permanent abode within us. But once we have realisation, it becomes part and parcel of our life and lasts for Eternity.

How do you know that there is such a thing as realisation, and how do you know when you are realised?

Many people have realised God. This is not my theory; this is not my discovery. Indian sages, Indian spiritual Masters of the hoary past, have discovered the Truth; and I also see eye to eye with them on the strength of my own realisation.

When you eat a mango, you know that you have eaten it. You have eaten a mango and the knowledge of it remains inside you. If others say, "No, you have not eaten a mango," it does not bother you, for you know what you have done. As long as your hunger is satisfied, you do not need the approval or recognition of others. The delicious taste, the experience that you had, is proof enough for you. In the spiritual world also, when one has drunk the Nectar of realisation, one knows that one has really realised God. One feels infinite Peace, infinite Light, infinite Bliss, infinite Power in his inner consciousness. A realised person can see, feel and know what Divinity is in his own inner consciousness. When one has realisation, he has a free access to God and a sense of complete fulfilment. When realisation dawns in an aspirant's life, then he will know it unmistakably.

How to know
When you have realised God?
The day you can look in the mirror
And use your inner will-power
To see not only your face
But countless other faces
In and around your face,
And know that these faces
Are all yours—
On that day you will know
That you have realised God.

Is it certain that every human being will be realised and earth will be illumined?

It is absolutely certain that everybody will become realised. Not only will every human being become realised, but also all the souls that are in the animal kingdom will eventually come into the human kingdom, and then they too will become realised. No creation of God will remain unrealised and unillumined. Earth will definitely be illumined; it is only a matter of time. God's entire creation has to realise God. This is God's Decree. Otherwise, God's Game will not be complete.

God's Heart-Door
Is always wide open
For you to come and go,
But if you are wise,
You will come only to stay.

What is the difference between a mystical experience and God-realisation?

God-realisation is infinitely higher than a mystical experience. In a mystical experience, you feel God's Presence as something very sweet and delicate, but a mystical experience is not permanent. As soon as you achieve a mystical experience, you can lose it. But God-realisation is permanent. Once you realise God, you never lose what you have.

A mystic is much inferior to a yogi. There is no comparison. A mystic is satisfied with experiences alone. He wants to enter into wisdom-light, but he does not care for the world. The mystic wants only the experience which leads to a final merging in God. A yogi constantly and unconditionally serves the Supreme and at the same time is continuously having God-experiences.

Since God is within us and we know that one day we will realise God, why is it necessary to practise Yoga?

One day we shall realise everything which is natural. God is natural and so naturally we shall realise Him. But those who do not practise spiritual discipline will have to wait for Eternity to realise God. God has given us a conscious mind and conscious aspiration. If we do not want to use our conscious aspiration, then we can wait. God is not compelling us or forcing us. We can sleep if we want to. But if we consciously pray and meditate, then we will realise God sooner. Everybody will reach the Goal, but he who sleeps will not reach the Goal as fast as he who is running. One day everybody will realise God because in God's Cosmic Vision, He will never allow anyone to remain unrealised. But it will take a very long time.

Why does God make it so difficult for those who aspire to realise Him?

God has not made it difficult for the sincere seekers. For the sincere seekers, the road is very short. Only for the doubtful seekers is the road very long. This moment you may feel that God is very kind to you, but the next moment you get a blow or some pain and then you lose faith. Some unconscious part of you may say, "O God, why are You so cruel to me? This morning I meditated so well. How is it that my body is now suffering?" At that time if you can say, "Although I am suffering such pain, perhaps something infinitely more serious was going to happen to me and God saved me. God is so kind to me," if you can change your attitude towards God, immediately the road becomes easier.

The road is long only for those who do not feel gratitude to God. If something bad happens, immediately think, "Oh, it could have been infinitely worse. Because of His infinite Compassion, God has not allowed something worse to come." If you have that kind of attitude, then the road becomes very, very easy.

God is ready to give you
Instant realisation.
Will you be able to receive it
With your constant aspiration?

In one of your books you said, "If you want to see God, you have to meditate twelve hours a day. If you want to come face to face with God, you have to meditate twenty-four hours a day." Is that possible?

When you are on the verge of realisation, it is quite possible, because at that time you have acquired considerable capacity. Even while you are eating, while you are talking, while you are doing your job, you will be having your best meditation. At that time, you will be able to do many things at a time. After you make considerable progress in your inner life, you will see that your inner being is meditating twenty-four hours a day.

What do you think is the greatest obstacle in achieving God-realisation?

The greatest obstacle need not be the same for each individual. Somebody's greatest obstacle will be doubt; somebody else may have fear as his greatest obstacle, and a third person may have insecurity. All these difficulties can be overcome by using only one weapon and that is love.

Let us take obstacles as imperfections. A child plays in the playground and gets covered with mud and dirt. Then he just runs to his mother, and she cleans him. It is the bounden duty of the mother to clean the child. If the child feels that because he is dirty his mother will scold him, insult him and strike him, then he will not go to her. But he does not feel that. First of all, he does not consider himself dirty. Then, when he runs to his mother, he is aware only of her love. He feels that his mother is his all. At every moment he has a free access to her.

If we have doubt, if we have fear, if we have other undivine qualities or imperfections, like a child let us run toward our eternal Father. He is there to purify us, to illumine us, to liberate us, to give us what He has. We have a free access to the eternal Father. But if we use our physical mind, we will feel, "Oh, God will be displeased with us. God will not accept us because we are so dirty, so imperfect, so impure."

The physical mind immediately separates us. It makes us feel that we are all imperfection while God is perfect Perfection; so how can we go to Him? But if we feel that God is our very own, that God is all Love for us and we are all Love for Him, then we just go and place ourselves at His Feet. At that time, there is no obstacle.

My first impression of God:
He is infinitely more indulgent
Than I thought.

We have to feel that what God is, we also are.
That very thing we are right now, but we are not
aware of it. We have to feel that God has created
us and He wants us to grow into His very image.
We have a mind which separates us; but we also
have a heart. When the heart comes to the fore,
immediately we feel tremendous joy, relief and
satisfaction. We feel that God is ours. When we
use our heart, we claim God as our very own on
the strength of our oneness. When we use the
heart, there is no obstacle which cannot be sur-
mounted. As a child has established his oneness
with the mother, even so we can establish our
oneness with God on the strength of our spontaneous love for Him.

God-realisation means God-discovery,
And God-discovery is nothing other than
The reclaiming of one's own
Ancient God-roots.

When someone reaches God-realisation, what happens to his soul?

The realised soul remains with the body. If the soul remains in the body when a person is realised, then he can consciously work for the divinity in humanity. He will feel at that time that he is a conscious instrument of God, that God is the Doer and God is the Action and that God is utilising him. When the veil of ignorance is removed, the soul gets the greatest opportunity to fulfil God's Mission on earth.

Is it necessary to come into contact with an enlightened person in order to realise God?

It is not necessary or obligatory to have a living Master. But if we have a living Master, it may help us considerably. The first person who realised God did it without the help of any human being. God Himself gave him God-realisation. But if we have a living Master, then we have more confidence in ourselves. We are more convinced.

As we need teachers for our outer knowledge, so also we need a spiritual Master to help and guide us in our inner life, especially in the beginning. Otherwise, our progress will be very slow and uncertain. The Master will encourage and inspire the seeker and give him the proper explanations of his experiences. Again, if the seeker is doing something wrong in his meditation, the Master will be in a position to correct him.

Why does one go to the university when one can study at home? It is because he feels that he will get expert instruction from people who know the subject well. There are exceptions, of course. There have been a few—very, very few—men of knowledge who did not go to any university. God is in everybody, and if a seeker feels that he does not need human help, he is most welcome to try his capacity alone. But if someone is wise and wants to run towards his Goal, instead of stumbling or merely walking, then certainly the help of a Guru can be considerable.

Let us say that I am in London. I know that New York exists and that I have to go back there. What do I need to get me there? An airplane and a pilot. In spite of the fact that I know that New York exists, I cannot get there alone. Similarly, you know that God exists. You want to reach God, but someone has to take you there. As the airplane takes me to New York, someone has to carry you to the Consciousness of God which is deep within you. Someone has to show you how to enter into your own divinity, which is God.

For millennia we have been swimming in the sea of ignorance. When we become awakened, we want to swim across the sea into the ocean of Light and Delight. If we know that there is a boatman with a boat which can safely carry us to our goal, then naturally we will try to get help from him. A genuine spiritual Master knows the way and is bound to help us reach the goal. Like a boatman, he will carry us to the other shore.

In human life, if people see that someone has taken help, they may say, "Oh, he could not do it alone." But a person who is really hungry for God will say, "No matter who offers the food, I am hungry and I want to eat immediately. This is the food that I have been crying for all my life and he is supplying me with it. As long as he is feeding true Divinity to me, let me eat."

CHAPTER EIGHT

God's Love

God loves us. He loves us constantly and unconditionally. No matter what we have done, what we are doing or what we shall do, He will always love us. God loves us much more than He loves Himself. If we use our thinking and doubting minds, this may seem hard to believe. But if we use our loving and surrendering hearts, then we are bound to feel that God loves us infinitely more than He loves Himself. Why does He love us so much? He loves us because He feels that His Dream remains unfulfilled without us, His Reality remains unmanifested without us; without us, He is incomplete.

There have been many, many times in our lives when we have felt miserable because we told a lie or deceived someone or became jealous of others. After we do something wrong, our conscience comes to the fore and we feel miserable.

We curse ourselves and try to punish ourselves. But God's Love for us remains exactly the same. We hate ourselves for our mistakes, but God still loves us and will always continue to love us. Our justice-power condemns us, but God's Compassion-Power forgives us, illumines us and transforms our weakness into strength. God gets satisfaction when, with His blessingful Smile, He gives us His Compassion-Flood, His Concern-Sky and His Love-Sea so that we can grow into His very image.

God loves us, and in return He wants us to smile, to love and to transcend. The moment we offer Him a soulful smile, God is pleased with us. The moment we offer Him an iota of our love, God is pleased with us. The moment we want to transcend our earth-bound consciousness, God is pleased with us.

Our human love constantly tries to separate and divide, but the divine Love we get from God always adds and multiplies. God used His Delight-Power when He created the world, and now He uses His Love-Power to protect the world and bring perfection to earth, His creation.

God gives us what He has and what He is. What He has is infinite Peace, Light and Bliss, and what He is is His constant Concern— Concern for our liberation from the meshes of ignorance and Concern for our perfection. God loves us. We love God. By loving God, we gain victory over our age-old ignorance. By loving us, God makes us consciously feel that we are eternal players, divine players in His Cosmic Game.

God definitely loves me
No matter what I am doing,
But He will definitely love me
Infinitely more
If He sees me dreaming
Of becoming another God
Like Him.

Love is the inner bond, the inner connection, the inner link between man and God, between the finite and the Infinite. We always have to approach God through love. Without love, we cannot become one with God. If we go through our journey with absolute love, we can never fail to reach God or fulfil Him, either in our own lives or in humanity.

What is love? If love means possessing someone or something, then that is not real love; that is not true love. If love means giving and becoming one with everything, with humanity and divinity, then that is real love. Real love is our total one-ness with the object loved and with the possessor of love. Who is the possessor of love? God.

Whom are we loving? We are loving the Su-preme in each individual. When we love the body, we bind ourselves; when we love the soul, we free ourselves. It is the soul in the individual, the Su-preme in each human being, that we have to love.

Nothing can be greater than love. God is great only because He has infinite Love. If we want to define God, we can define Him in mil-lions of ways, but I wish to say that no definition of God can be as adequate as the definition of God as all Love. When we say 'God', if fear comes into our mind, then we are millions and billions of miles away from Him. When we repeat the name of God, if love comes to the fore, then our prayer, our concentration, our meditation, our contemplation are genuine. There can be no greater wisdom, no greater knowledge, than love.

The world exists just because love still exists on earth. If this one divine quality left the world, then there could be no existence on earth. No other divine quality can create, sustain and fulfil God here on earth like the quality of love. Divine love does not mean an emotional exchange of human thoughts or ideas; it means the fulfilment of oneness.

How do I know that God loves me?

The Supreme has given you as a human being the capacity and potentiality to realise Him. If He is not kind, why has He given you this human life? He has given you this life, He has given you the aspiration, He has given you the opportunity and He has given you the capacity to realise His highest Height. Would He have given you all this if He did not love you? The Supreme does love you. That is why He has given you the aspiration to seek His Love.

If you think the Supreme does not love you, you have to know that you are a real fool. It is the Supreme who has created love. He has created your very existence. It is like a gardener who has created a garden with many beautiful flowers. If a flower says, "No, no, he does not love me!" is that not ridiculous? The very fact that the gardener has planted and cultivated the flowers—is this not his love? At every moment you have to feel that the Supreme does love you. Otherwise, He would not have brought you into His creation.

God loves you
For your heart's
Aspiration-purity.

God loves you
For your life's
Dedication-intensity.

God loves you
For your soul's
Omnipresent luminosity.

What is the difference between human love and divine love?

Human love is very limited. In human love, there is every possibility of being captured by pleasure. In human love, there is practically no opportunity to expand our divine consciousness. True human love, even if it is not spiritual, will have some psychic emotion in it. This emotion will try to show us that love should not bind or impose. However, in human love we always feel that the other person does not want us or need us. There is always some fear or hatred in human love. Human love, as everybody knows, ends in frustration, and frustration is followed by destruction. In human love, we end up losing our own sweet feeling of oneness with the other person and we end up losing our divine reality.

Divine love makes no demand. It is spontaneous and constant. It is unlimited in every way. It is like the sun. The sun is for everybody. Everybody can use the sunlight, but if we keep our doors and windows shut, what can the sun do? It is God's divine Love that has to act in and through human love. But if we do not care for the divine love that is flowing around us or wants to flow in us, then the divine love cannot function in and through us.

Human love binds; but before it binds it is already bound. Divine love illumines, but before it illumines, we see that it is already illumined. Divine love starts with the awareness of a higher reality. It is our constant conviction of a very high truth. Divine love at every moment illumines us, and in illumination we see total fulfilment.

God unconditionally loves
Each and every human being.
Indeed, this is a divine mystery
That no human mind can ever fathom.

The very nature of human love is to stick only to one person and to reject everyone else. But in divine love, which is unlimited and infinite, the question of acceptance and rejection does not arise at all. In divine love there is no possession, but only a feeling of oneness. This oneness can enter into an animal, into a flower, into a tree or even into a wall. It is not like human love where today we want to possess one person or thing, tomorrow two persons, the day after tomorrow, three. When we have divine love for someone, at that time there is automatically inseparable oneness. No bridge is required; we just become one.

Divine love tells us that our life is infinitely more important than we imagine. Divine love means constant transcendence, not only of our human boundaries, but of God's own Realisation in and through us.

In divine love, we grow. Divine love, the love of the soul, liberates and expands our consciousness. Love means oneness of divinity, oneness of reality, oneness of the individual consciousness with the unlimited Consciousness. When we enter into the Universal Consciousness through our meditation, we do not think of human love. We think only of divine love and oneness. If we have something small like a tiny knife, then we cannot cut something very big with it. But if we have a very big knife, then we can cut something large with it. The instrument that we are using right now is our very limited consciousness. That is why we are limited in our love. But if we use the other instrument, which is very vast, if we use the Universal Consciousness, our capacity for divine love becomes unlimited.

Divine love will come from God and from our own meditation, but only when we do not cherish expectation. A child expects either a penny or a nickel or a quarter from his father. More than that is beyond his expectation. If he expects from his father all the time, the father will give, but he will give only what the child expects. But if the child feels that whatever his father has is also his, and if he wants only to please his father, then when the father feels that the child is capable of receiving it, he will give the child all his wealth.

I am just learning to feel
That I do not have to actually catch God,
But that someday God will catch me
And pour into my heart
A flood of ineffable Delight.

When we do not expect anything from God, God will give us everything. He will say, "It is I who am giving the infinite Love. How is it that My children remain with very limited capacity, very limited achievement?" In order to prove that He and His children are one, that we are His worthy instruments, He will give us His infinite Peace, Light and Bliss.

When one becomes unconditionally surrendered to God's Will, one gets infinite divine love. Everything will come in the form of love. We will get peace, but it will come in the form of love; and this peace we will offer to mankind through love. Just because we love, we are spreading our peace or power. God Himself manifests everything through Love. Here on earth and there in Heaven, there is only one thing that God is proud of, and that is Love, divine Love.

We pray to God the Power
But God the Lover
Answers our prayers.

How can we feel that God loves us infinitely more than we love ourselves?

The proof of the pudding is in the eating itself. The human in us feels that we are either the lowest or the highest. When it identifies with the lowest, it says, "I am useless, I am nothing." In this way the vital comes forward and tries to gain sympathy. Each time a doubt comes and we feel that we are not God's instrument, we fall short of our capacity. How many times we doubt ourselves, belittle ourselves, kill ourselves! The moment we doubt that God is inside us, a dark spot appears on the golden tablet of our heart. When we do not love ourselves, the face of the sun is covered with clouds. The moment we belittle our capacity and doubt ourselves, the moment we forget what we eternally are, at that time we are millions of miles from the truth. We love ourselves only when we feel that we have achieved something or feel that tomorrow or the day after we are going to do something. This is the human in us.

God is our highest part, our most illumined part. When we enter into our highest consciousness and know that we are in all, of all and for all, at that time we do not doubt ourselves. At that time, we are everything, so who can doubt whom? We embody God and want to reveal and manifest

God, so we do not even dream of minimising our capacity. Here we are spontaneously embodying and revealing the divine.

When the real, the highest, the most illumined part in us comes to the fore, at that time we really love ourselves. We love ourselves because we know who we are. Love is not a kind of outer movement or action. Love is life, and life itself is spontaneous nectar and delight. So the Supreme in us, who is infinite Delight, loves us infinitely more than we love ourselves.

It appears to me that God's Love is conditional, that it depends on whether I meditate and aspire properly or not, or whether I am appreciating it.

Unfortunately, here you are making a mistake. Divine Love is not conditional; it does not depend on what you do. The reason you feel this way is because you do not empty your vessel. When you empty your inner vessel, you will see that love is flowing through you, and then you will feel that your vessel is full to the brim. God's Love does not depend on what you do except in this sense: if you keep the door wide open, then the Highest can enter. But if you do not open your inner door, it is impossible for the highest Reality to enter into you.

Everything that comes from God is unconditional. His Love He gives unconditionally, but somebody has to receive it. The sunlight is unconditional; everybody can receive it. But if you remain fast asleep, if you do not want to open up the windows and doors, then for you there is no sunlight.

I don't understand why God's Love doesn't enter into me even though I keep the doors shut.

If God's Love enters into you when you are not receptive to it, then you will regard it as a foreign element. You will not appreciate it or care for it. If somebody brings most delicious food right in front of you but you do not appreciate it, then you will just discard it and feel that it has no value.

I may not know
What is in God's Mind,
But I do know
What is in God's Heart:
Unconditional Love for me.

Mine is the mind
That is bewildered.
Mine is the heart
That is broken.
Mine is the vital
That is bruised.
Mine is the soul
That is aching.
My Lord,
Yet I feel
That You love me,
Yet I know
That You care for me.

The love that spans the universe
Is not new.
It is old,
Ancient
And eternal.

CHAPTER NINE

God's Compassion

Man's heartbeat
Is God's purest Compassion.
God's Heartbeat
Is man's surest transformation.

Compassion is God's immense and intense Concern for mankind. When we show compassion to others at the time of their need, compassion is sweet. When we receive compassion from others while we are in dire need, compassion is sweeter. And when we come to realise that it is God's Compassion that is enabling us to fulfil our promise both to Heaven and to earth, Compassion is sweetest. Our promise to Heaven is to reveal our divine qualities here on earth. Our promise to earth is to manifest all our divine capacities so that Mother-Earth can utilise them for her own purposes.

We feel that if we can receive God's most illumining Compassion, then our spiritual journey will be expedited. But how are we going to receive this Compassion from Above? We can easily do it if we can feel that we are a child, a little divine child. When a human child cries, no matter where the mother is, she comes to comfort him, for by pleasing the child she gets satisfaction. Similarly, when we soulfully cry for God's Compassion, God immediately descends with His Compassion-Power.

A child cries helplessly because he feels that without his mother's help and guidance he cannot do anything. But the spiritual child does not cry with a sense of helplessness. He feels that there is a Source, and that Source is omniscient, omnipotent and omnipresent. When we become soulful in our cry, we establish a free access to the Source. So the seeker in us, the divine child in us, cries soulfully and not helplessly.

Compassion wants to operate in us at every moment, but quite often, because of our ignorance, we resist Compassion consciously or unconsciously, even after we have begun to cry for it. In the ordinary life, if somebody wants to give us something out of his infinite kindness, and we do not take it, then the person immediately withdraws his gift, as if to say that we do not deserve it. But God never withdraws His Compassion from us. On the contrary, He tries to offer more of His divine, unconditional Compassion.

Compassion is a power, an illumining power. But when we are extremely stubborn and reject Compassion totally and mercilessly, God at times relies on His Patience-Power. He knows that Eternity is at His disposal and that one day in the process of evolution we shall be able to receive His Compassion. Today if we do not achieve and receive His Compassion devotedly or gratefully, He does not mind. Tomorrow He will give us another opportunity, and in either the near or the distant future, we are bound to accept His Compassion-Power, for this alone can transform our nature. So God does not withdraw; He only uses another type of power, which we call patience.

Temptation grips man,
Compassion grips God:
This is God's and man's
Absolutely most
Ancient story.

God's greatest gift to mankind is His Compassion, and man's greatest gift to God is his surrender. When man surrenders to God soulfully and unconditionally, when he surrenders to God's Will cheerfully, at that time God's Capacity, God's Reality, God's Infinitude become his. Compassion is the magnet in God, and surrender is the magnet in the seeker. When God uses His Compassion, it is like a magnet from above pulling us up to the Highest. And when we use our surrender, this magnet immediately pulls God down into our living breath. So when our magnet and God's magnet come together, the Hour of God dawns for us in our life of aspiration and self-dedication.

If you have the sincere courage
To declare that you are
Totally lost,
Then God has the unreserved Compassion
To show you the way
To the Satisfaction-Goal.

Is God's Compassion the same as His Love?

God's Love is for everybody. It is like the sun. A person has only to keep open the window of his heart to receive divine Love. When God's Love takes an intimate form, it is called Compassion. This Compassion is the most powerful attribute, the most significant attribute of the Supreme.

God's Compassion is for the selected few. God's Compassion is like a magnet that pulls the aspirant toward his goal. It is a mighty force that guides, pushes and pulls the aspirant constantly and does not allow him to slip on the path of self-realisation. God's Love comforts and helps the aspirant, but if the aspirant falls asleep, the Divine Love will not force him to awaken and compel him to resume his journey.

God's Compassion is not like human compassion. In a human way we can have compassion and pity for somebody, but this compassion does not have the strength to change the person and make him run from his ignorant condition toward the Light. In the case of God's Compassion, it is a force that changes and transforms the aspirant and keeps him from making major mistakes in his spiritual life.

Love can stay even with ignorance, but Compassion will not. Compassion has to be successful; otherwise it may be withdrawn. It will stay for a few seconds, or for a few minutes or a few years; but it has to send a report to the highest Authority and say whether it has been successful or not. A time may come when the highest Authority

says, "It is a barren desert. Come back." Then
Compassion has to fly back to the highest Authority, the Supreme.

Even before I knew
Who God was,
God started painting my life
With His Compassion-Colours.

The Supreme is omniscient, omnipotent and
omnipresent. He has various kinds of Power, but
His greatest adamantine Power is His Grace. The
moment the Supreme uses His Grace for an individual, He offers His very Life-Breath to the
seeker, for the Supreme and His Grace can never
be separated. Whenever we think of the Supreme,
if we feel that it is through His Grace that we are
approaching Him, then we can be most successful in receiving Him.

The divine Grace is constantly descending
upon us. Those who are sincerely aspiring are
conscious of this divine Grace, but those who are
not aspiring are keeping their heart's door permanently closed. If we feel that the Supreme is
Grace, then we shall see that His infinite qualities, Peace, Light and Bliss, are already in the
process of entering into us, ceaselessly flowing in
and through us and becoming part and parcel of

our inner and outer life. We have only to allow the flow of Grace to carry us into the Source, which is the Supreme.

God's Grace is like the rays of the sun. The sun is always there, but what do we do? We get up late. Instead of getting up at five-thirty or six o'clock, we get up at eight or nine o'clock. Then we do not get the blessing of the morning sun. And when we do get up, we keep the doors and windows all shut and do not allow the sunlight to enter into our room.

Similarly, God's Grace is constantly descending, but quite often we are not allowing the Grace to enter into our system. We have kept barriers between God's Grace and our own ignorance. Only if we keep our heart's door wide open can God's Light enter into our existence. God's Light means God's Grace. There is no difference between God's Grace and God's Compassion-Light.

Every day we have to empty our inner vessel and fill it with God's Peace, Light and Bliss. We have to feel that God's Light is there all the time and is more than willing to illumine us. Then only we will be able to utilise God's Grace. Again, if we miss God's Grace, we should not be doomed to disappointment. Today we have not allowed the sunlight to enter into our room, but tomorrow again the sun will be there. If today we have not allowed God's Grace to enter into us due to our ignorance, no harm. Tomorrow we will definitely be prepared for God's Light to enter into us.

What does God's Compassion do when we resist God's Grace?

Compassion and Grace are the same thing, but Compassion is much more intense. The same Grace, when it has tremendous intensity, is called Compassion. Water is everywhere, but when there is a torrential rain, you can say Compassion is descending. It is like a heavy downpour from Above, with tremendous force. Grace is also water, but water is here, there, everywhere. This is the difference between Compassion and Grace.

When an individual resists God's Compassion, God either waits indefinitely and uses His Patience-Power, or He uses more Compassion. In His case He deals with infinite Compassion. He does not accept any defeat. If we resist His

Compassion, He may use more of His Compassion to conquer us, or He may allow us to stay for ten, twenty, fifty, sixty or a hundred years more in ignorance. He is dealing with eternal Time.

It is up to Him whether to force us to accept His Light in a different way. But this forcing does not occur in a human way. His forcing means that He will use more of the Compassion-Power which He has and which He is. From His infinite Compassion, He will use more Compassion in order to conquer our ignorance. But if He meets with tremendous resistance, then He may change His mind. He may say, "No, he wants to sleep; let him sleep for another hundred years. There is no hurry in it."

God will never withdraw His Compassion for good, no matter how we resist His Compassion. Only we delay our onward, upward, inward progress by resisting God's Compassion-Power. For God's Compassion-Power is His magnetic Power that draws us to His very Heart, which is all Light and Delight.

My heart's iota of suffering
Can never, never equal
The Compassion-Flood
That descends from Above
Not only to console me
But also to illumine
And satisfy me.

Can God's Grace change fate?

Fate can and must be changed. For that, what is required is God's Grace plus personal effort. There are some seekers who feel, "If I care for God's Grace, what necessity is there to make personal effort?" But they are mistaken. Personal effort will never stand in the way of God's descending Grace. Personal effort expedites the descent of God's Grace.

God can give us all that He wants without even an iota of personal effort from us. He says, "It is for your own satisfaction that I ask you to make this little personal effort." When we can make this personal effort, our whole life will be surcharged with divine pride: "See what I have done for God!" Our conscious oneness with God, who is infinite, who is eternally immortal, prompts us to do something for our Dearest and not for our ego.

If we sincerely make personal effort, God is bound to be thrilled with us. Why? Because He can tell the world, "My child, My chosen instrument, has done this for Me and that for Me." Through personal effort we can make our existence on earth worthy and, at the same time, we can make God proud of us.

Ultimately, personal effort has to grow into a dynamic self-surrender. When we offer the results of our aspiration and inner urge to God, that is called true surrender. If we do not offer the results to God and just lie like a dead body at His Feet, letting Him work for us, in us and through us, it is wrong. God does not want an inactive body, a dead soul. He wants someone who is active, dynamic and aspiring; someone who wants to be energised so that he can do something for God; someone who wants to realise God and manifest all the divine qualities here on earth.

Surrender is our ultimate achievement. There is no difference between God's Grace and our unconditional surrender. God's Grace and our unconditional surrender are like the obverse and reverse of the same coin. If God did not give us that kind of Grace, then we could not make unconditional surrender. To receive God's Grace is a real achievement. To make unconditional surrender is also a real achievement.

How do I know if I have done something through personal effort or through God's Grace?

You have to know that Grace is something we can never understand and will never understand unless and until we have realised God. Personal effort is also God's Grace. There are many stories about how seekers think it is all personal effort and later come to realise that it was all God's Grace. As long as we are not aware of God's constant Grace, we have to use our personal effort.

God has been crying for us as individuals to come out of the sea of ignorance. God's Grace is responsible for everything, but before we can feel it, it is always advisable for us to make a conscious personal effort. If we do not consciously make a personal effort, then we will never be able to know what God's Grace is. After we have realised the highest Truth, we shall see that personal effort is nothing but God's hidden Grace.

Without the Grace-Power,
Everything is out of reach.
With the Grace-Power,
Everything is within easy reach.

There is a fixed hour when God will kindle our consciousness whether we have faith in Him or not. He waits for the choice hour and when the hour strikes, He comes and gives us what He wants to give. But that does not mean that we shall not aspire, that we shall live in the world of sleep and not make any personal effort. No! We shall go on like a true farmer and cultivate the soil with sincere dedication and regularity, and after we do our part, we will leave it up to God to decide when He wants to give us the bumper crop of realisation.

An atom of soulful effort:
God comes down.
A second of self-giving cry:
Look, God is happily watching you.

CHAPTER TEN

God's Justice

In the ordinary human life, justice says, "As you sow, so you reap." This is justice: tit for tat. If somebody has done something wrong, we feel we have every right to threaten him, frighten him and punish him. But this kind of justice is on the lowest rung of the human ladder. When we step up to a higher rung, justice becomes forgiveness. If we can forgive someone who has done something wrong, that forgiveness itself is justice.

Divine Justice is ready at every moment to be of help to us, to inspire us, guide us, mould us and shape us. But we are equally afraid of divine Justice and human justice. When we do something wrong, we feel that we will be exposed. This is true in the case of human justice. But divine Justice will never, never expose us. The first time we do something wrong, divine Justice will forgive us with its Compassion. The second time we do something wrong, it will offer us more Compassion. The third time we do something wrong, it will offer us infinite Compassion. Then, when the Supreme sees that even His infinite Compassion is not solving the human problem, He will use His loving, divine Authority, His divine Power.

This divine Power is not a destructive power. It is not a threatening power. This divine Power awakens the dormant lion in each human being. Divine Power does not dominate. It only arouses the spiritually hungry lion in each human being. The lion can roar, but the lion is fast asleep. This lion embodies our inner cry to see the ultimate Truth, to grow into the Absolute Reality.

Today my Lord Supreme is telling me
That His Compassion
Is absolutely free of charge
And His Justice borders on indulgence.
I am all eagerness
To have them both
In abundant measure.

When we enter into the highest level of consciousness, there is no question of either punishment or forgiveness. It is only a matter of illumination. The highest Self encompasses and embodies all of Reality. So if one part of its existence is unillumined, it does not punish or forgive. It tries to illumine that part of its own existence. When we see the world from the highest plane of consciousness, we feel that the ignorant, obscure, impure, imperfect world needs illumination. Here, justice is the feeling of oneness. Divine Justice is the transformation of our own unlit existence. Divine Justice is self-illumination.

Divine Justice is nothing short of divine Forgiveness. Human justice says that if somebody has stolen something, he has to be punished. Human justice tells us that this is the right thing, and it gets tremendous pleasure by punishing the person. But when divine Justice operates, even if it takes an outer form, inside this Justice there is tremendous compassion. While the inner judge is telling the world that so-and-so is the culprit, he is illumining the person's mind so that he does not enter into ignorance again. When divine Justice is offered, there is an inner compassion and an inner illumination inside it. They work together so the seeker does not fall again and again into the sea of ignorance.

When human justice operates, the culprit does not feel that anybody else has instigated him. He feels that he has been responsible all the time. Divine Justice helps the culprit realise that it is not he who has committed the wrong act, but something else, which we call ignorance, which has operated in and through him.

When divine Justice operates, the person feels miserable that he has allowed some wrong forces to enter into him and act in and through him. He feels he was a fool to allow somebody or something else to operate in and through him. He realises he should act only according to his own soul's divine guidance.

> *God's Compassion*
> *Forgives us.*
> *God's Justice*
> *Illumines us.*

Why does it sometimes seem that God's Justice does not give the same opportunity to everyone?

When we see that someone is not getting the same amount of peace, light or bliss from God, we have to feel that the Supreme is giving to each one according to his capacity or his receptivity. The Supreme is always doing justice to the inferior one, to the one who is still in a preliminary stage. But at the same time, He is all Love for that person. He does not want that person's inner vessel to burst untimely. If you ask, "Why is the Supreme not playing His Game justly? Why is He giving so much peace and power to one person and not to another?" the answer is that one person is not ready. Whatever He is giving to each person is a sign of His Love. He will say, "You are My infant, My child, and I can give you this much. This is what is required." If the Supreme gives him more than that, He may ruin the inner progress of that individual. But the one who is given more has the capacity to receive it, to embody it and to fulfil it.

In the ordinary life, we feel that equality is justice. But in the divine life, if somebody has the capacity to receive more peace, more light, more bliss from Above, then he should be given more. Equal opportunity should be given, but if you have more capacity or receptivity than I have, then you should progress according to your own speed and not slow down to my speed. If you wait for me, then God's Hour will have to wait for you, and you will not reach the Goal at God's choice Hour.

This kind of equality is not an act of illumination. If your time has come, you go. God has given me the same opportunity, but you have developed more capacity. That is why you have received more light and you can run faster toward your Goal. When God gives me the capacity at His choice Hour, at that time I also will reach the Goal. This is called divine Justice. God is constantly giving us all the same opportunity, but our individual capacity is not the same.

What does God's Justice do when jealousy and impurity are brought before the Supreme's Court?

God's Justice is not human justice; it is not punishment. God only says, "I have given you chances time and again, but you have not properly used the golden Hour. Again, I am ready to give chances endlessly." At that time God deals with His infinite Patience. First He deals with Light. He tries to illumine our jealousy and impurity and transform them into a feeling of oneness and purity.

But if the seeker does not want his jealousy or impurity to be illumined, then God uses another weapon: His Patience-weapon. The first weapon he uses is His Wisdom-weapon. Patience also is a form of wisdom, and wisdom is patience, but we separate them.

Suppose you are a selfish person. God says, "The moment you forget about your personal, selfish, self-seeking life and care only for self-giving, then your jealousy will go away. The moment you pay attention only to purity, then impurity will leave you." First this wisdom God will try to shower on you. But if you do not avail yourself of this opportunity to receive God's Wisdom, then God will use another weapon which is called His Patience. He will wait until you feel the necessity of purification and transformation of your nature.

Then, after ten years or twenty years or fifty years, again He will try to inspire you. At that time, if He succeeds, well and good. Otherwise, there will be another time. In this way continuously He will go on, go on, go on. In the course of time, the seeker will fulfil the demands of his inner being and God's Promise to His own Reality.

My Lord Supreme,
You forgive me
And give me another chance,
Not because
I deserve forgiveness
But because
You want Your entire creation
To be absolutely perfect.

Is force excluded in divine Justice?

The Supreme uses force, but it is not human force. Beating or striking someone, showing supremacy or authority: this is human force. But the Supreme's Force operates in a different way. His Force is the intensity of necessity. Suppose the seeker is not intense in his aspiration. The Supreme will make him intense. This intensity you can call force, but it is not thrust upon him. Somebody is lethargic. He wants to go slowly, at the speed of an Indian bullock cart. But God says, "Now I have invented the jet plane. Why do you have to use an Indian bullock cart?"

So God will use His Intensity-Power. This Intensity we may misunderstand. We may think that God is forcing us, that He is compelling us to go. No, He is just awakening us. He just says, "Look, open your eyes. Here is the fastest speed." When He awakens our consciousness, we feel that it has been done by pressure. But if we are sincere, devoted and surrendered, we do not feel any kind of pressure; we only feel that the time has come. God has selected a choice Hour and He has awakened us.

In human force there is a compulsion. The force is coming to frighten us, to threaten us. But when there is force in divine Justice, it does not frighten or threaten us. It only increases the intensity of our aspiration so that, like a bullet, we run towards the goal. When God uses force, God will ask us to run towards the goal at the pace that He has set, not at our pace. If we do not identify ourselves with God's Will, then it really becomes a kind of pressure, a force. But if we become one with Him, then there is no pressure or force.

O fearful heart,
Do believe that God does not know
How to punish.
God knows only how to illumine
And thus satisfy His Eternity's
Infinite Vision-Dreams.

What is your view of the part of the Bible that says we should fear God's Justice?

You have to forgive me, but I cannot subscribe to that view. We must not fear God's Justice and we must not fear God. If we fear God, we will never be able to reach God, we will never be able to get anything from God. If a child is afraid of his father, he will not be able to receive anything from his father. He will not even go to his father. If he sees that his father is so tall and robust and powerful, then he will not go to him. But if the child loves the father, even though the father has power and strength, the child feels that the father is not going to use it to strike him. On the contrary, the child feels that the father will use that power to protect him if he is in danger. The child feels that his father's power is all for him.

To approach God with fear or through fear is very unhealthy. We should only love God. We should feel that what our Father has, we also have. Unfortunately, we are still children; that is why our Father is unable to give it to us. The father does not give his vast wealth to a child. But when the child grows up, he gets what his father has and what his father is. If we can love God soulfully, then God will give us everything.

Do not fear.
He who fears cannot stay near
God's Compassion-Eye
And God's Forgiveness-Feet.

When a child is playing in the mud and then all of a sudden he is called, he is not afraid that his mother will beat him because he is dirty. He will go running to his mother and his mother will immediately take his dirt, his filth, as her very own. She will wash him in order to show others that her son is also very clean. We have to approach God like that. No matter how many undivine things we do, we can run toward Him and feel that with His Compassion He will clean us immediately.

Does God use force to make human beings listen to Him?

God is infinitely wiser than we are. Someone with less power than God may try to force another individual to do something that he does not want to do. But God does not force anyone to do anything. He feels that if He uses force, then we cannot get the ultimate joy.

You can force someone to eat, but inwardly he will curse you. God only says, "My child, I am telling you to eat this for your own good. If you eat this food, you will get nourishment. Then you will be strong and you will be able to fight against ignorance." God offers His Light, His inner nourishment, but He does not force anyone to accept it.

God sees the past, the present and the future. He knows that the right thing is to constantly offer us His Wisdom and infinite Patience. Human beings do not always have patience. They feel that by striking their child and by forcing him to do certain things, they are doing the best thing. But God the Father will not act in this way. He will only show infinite Compassion-Light. Then, in return, His child will eventually offer infinite gratitude to God. The child will receive this Compassion and he will try to become worthy of his Father.

Look at the power of a Justice of the Supreme Court when he is in his office. Again, when this same man is with his wife and children, he cannot exercise this kind of power. His own son may not listen to him. The Supreme Court Justice and the father are one and the same person. When he is in court, the whole nation listens to him, but at home his own children may not listen to him.

Similarly, when He is in Heaven, the Supreme is really the Highest and, at the same time, He is constantly transcending Himself. The Supreme has the supreme Power in the inner world. But when He wants to operate here on earth with His children, He uses infinite Patience. He becomes one with their ignorance and says, "All right, if you want to disobey Me, if you want to play these kinds of silly games, then let Me also play a little with you."

On earth God manifests not only Power but all His other qualities through Love. God can use His Power, but he prefers to manifest Himself through Love, Concern and Compassion.

If you open your heart,
You will feel that God
Can never be strict with you,
Never,
For His Compassion-Height
Is infinitely stronger
Than His Justice-Light.

How do God's and man's laws compare?

God's Law is operated by His Compassion-Light and man's law is operated by his judgement-might. When I do something wrong, human law tries to punish me, but punishment is not the ultimate answer. In the case of God's Law, when I do something wrong, for example when I steal, the Compassion of the Supreme will touch the root of my action and cause me to realise that stealing is wrong, that I should work for what I need and get it in a proper manner.

God's Compassion works in such a way as to help us change, while human law cannot change human nature. It is only divine Law, which is illumining, that can change and transform human nature. Human law is an immediate response to what you have done; it is action and reaction. Divine Law will enter into and transform the root of the ignorance.

Because so many violent things are happening in the world today, and because the world is so full of imperfection and quarrelling, many people say that God is angry with the world. Do you think God is angry with the world, or is He satisfied?

When we think of God as Compassion, as Love, we immediately feel that God is satisfied with us. But when we think of God as Justice, we feel that God is dissatisfied with us for our imperfection, our quarrelling, fighting and so forth. If we go deeper, we feel that God is all Love and that His Love is everywhere; it is all-pervading. It is His Love that pervades Heaven and earth.

God is Delight. From Delight the creation has come into existence, in Delight this world abides, and into Delight each individual soul will retire. If God is all Delight, if He is in Delight, then He cannot be angry with the creation. When somebody is in joy, in true joy, he does not find fault with anything or anybody.

Finally we come to see that it is not we who are actually doing anything. It is God who is the Doer and who is the action, and it is He who is having the experiences that we are seeing all around us. God the Compassion is not angry with us. God the Love is not dissatisfied with us, for it is He who is acting in and through us. He is the experience and He is the experiencer.

Even when
God's Justice descends,
It is accompanied by
His unseen Compassion.

CHAPTER ELEVEN

God's Forgiveness

O my life's Love Supreme,
Sleeplessly I invoke You
To forgive me today.
O great One, O world's reality-salvation,
May I be fully awakened
In purity's auspicious dawn.

How can I receive God's Forgiveness?

You can receive God's Forgiveness only by re-
minding yourself constantly, consciously, sleeplessly and breathlessly that God is Forgiveness
itself. You should not think of God as Justice or
infinite Light or Peace. You should not think of
any other aspect of God. You should only think of
God's Forgiveness or of God the Forgiveness.
You have to inundate your mind and your heart

with one thought: forgiveness, forgiveness, forgiveness. Instead of thinking of God's Justice-Light, you should just repeat: "My Lord is all Forgiveness, my Lord is all Forgiveness." While repeating, "My Lord is all Forgiveness," you must not think of all the countless undivine things that you have done. Only try to see the positive side. Think only of God's Forgiveness before you, around you and within you. If hundreds and thousands of times you can repeat most soulfully, "My Lord is all Forgiveness," then all your Himalayan blunders will be washed away. All the mistakes that you have made over the years, all the ignorant things that you have done, will be annihilated.

At that time, you will not only feel that you are forgiven, but you will feel that you yourself are God's Forgiveness. If someone asks you your name, you will say, "My name is my Lord's Forgiveness." If someone asks you who you are, you will say, "I am my Lord's Forgiveness." This will be your only credential. In the ordinary life people have many credentials. They have this university degree, that degree and so on. But a spiritual seeker will have only one credential. He will say "I am my Lord's Forgiveness," or "I am my Lord's Compassion," or "I am my Lord's Love." If somebody asks you what your credentials are, immediately you will say, "My Lord's Compassion is my only credential," or "My Lord's Forgiveness is my only credential." This is not just false humility, for in the inmost recesses of your heart you will feel that your only credential is God's Compassion or God's Forgiveness. This is what all seekers must feel.

In my outer life,
My Lord,
I see Your Compassion-Flood.
In my inner life,
My Lord,
I see Your Forgiveness-Ocean.

Should we pray to God for forgiveness?

When you make any mistake, consciously or unconsciously, immediately you should cry for forgiveness. If you do not ask the Supreme for forgiveness, then your own negative qualities will be intensified. With your aspiration, your prayer, your meditation, your dedication and your oneness with God's Will you have to ask God to forgive you for all your mistakes, conscious and unconscious. You have to ask Him to illumine your unconscious mistakes so that you will become aware of them and not make them again.

If your mistakes are not forgiven, you will never have purity in your heart, body, vital and mind and you will not be able to receive anything from God in these parts of your being. The soul is always receiving from God, because the soul is always pure. But the heart is not always pure and the body, vital and mind are all a dark jungle. If mistakes are not forgiven, then purification cannot take place in the body, vital, mind and heart. And if purity is not there, then the divine forces that you are praying for will never be able to enter permanently into your life. Only if God forgives your mistakes and you get purity in your entire consciousness will you be able to increase your receptivity and receive God's divine qualities in abundant measure.

The best thing is every day, before you go to sleep, to pray to the Supreme to forgive you for the things that you have done wrong. This is not the Christian philosophy that says we are all sinners. No, I am only speaking of the conscious or unconscious mistakes that you make in your daily life. You have to ask the Supreme to forgive you for these mistakes and to illumine your mistakes. Real forgiveness, illumination and purification always go together.

Sleeplessly I shall cry today
To see my Lord's
Forgiveness-Sweetness-Eye.

The Supreme illumines the past by forgiveness. Real forgiveness means forgetfulness, conscious forgetfulness. If somebody really forgives you for something that you did, then he will not keep the memory even in his inner vision. Illumination is necessary because of darkness. Mistakes are darkness. So the Supreme illumines our mistakes through forgiveness.

O Forgiver of all my shortcomings,
Forgive me.
A new hope is being born in my heart.
I shall cry from today on
To grow into Perfection's beauty-delight.

If a person feels that God is all-forgiving, won't that make it easier for the person to do the wrong thing?

You feel that if one goes to the Father after doing something wrong and sees that he is forgiven, then he will be tempted to keep doing wrong things, with the feeling that he will always be forgiven. Even the human father, not to speak of the divine Father, the Almighty Father, will tell the child, "Look, you have done something wrong; you have struck another child. Just because I love you, I have forgiven you, but you cannot go on doing wrong things." If the child for a second times strikes another child and then comes back to the father, the father will protect the child. Afterwards, secretly and silently the father will say, "This is the second time that I am telling you the difference between good and bad." Each time the father will forgive, but at the same time, he will try to convince the child that he is doing something wrong.

In the case of the divine Father, it is different. When the aspirant makes a mistake and runs toward the divine Father, the divine Father will forgive and protect the aspirant, without doubt. Then immediately the Father will try to enter into the heart of the aspirant with Light. The human father will scold secretly, but the divine Father will not scold; He knows that scolding is of no use. He tries to see what is wrong in the aspirant. He sees that darkness is there, ignorance is there, and says, "If I enter into the aspirant with Light, the Light will chase away the darkness. Then the Light will illumine the ignorance and transform it into knowledge and wisdom. This wisdom will make the aspirant feel that he should remain peaceful, calm, quiet, and not run into conflict with anybody." The divine Father accomplishes this by pouring Light into the aspirant.

The human father will protect openly and then scold secretly, but the divine Father will use pure Light to illumine our darkness and chase away the wrong forces in us. In both cases, the temptation will be conquered. The human father will conquer it through strict discipline, and the divine Father will conquer it through Light.

If I do something wrong and ask the Supreme to forgive me, how do I know whether He has forgiven me?

There are two ways you can know. If you never do that kind of thing again, rest assured that the Supreme has forgiven you, for He has given you the capacity not to do it again. On the practical level, if you have done something wrong and you do not want to do it again, that means that a higher Power has come from the Supreme to protect you and give you the capacity not to do the thing again. It is because the Supreme has forgiven you that you are not making that mistake anymore.

Another way is to ask your spiritual Master if the Supreme has forgiven you. The Master will be able to tell you. He will be very frank. Or you can go deep within for half an hour or an hour, and then you will be able to tell. Each time a thought comes, do not allow it to enter into your mind. Feel that a fly has come to sit on you, and chase it away. When another thought comes, chase it away too. After a while, the thought-fly will feel that it is beneath its dignity to bother you, and then the thought-process will stop. When you see that no thought is coming, just ask the question. If the answer is "yes," then it means that God has forgiven you.

There are two ways
To win forgiveness.
One way is to tell God,
"My Lord,
I shall not do it again!"
The other way is to ask God,
"My Lord,
Please show me the way
To live consciously in You
And for You."

How can we forgive injustice?

When we came into the world, we made a sincere, soulful and solemn promise to God that we would realise God, manifest God and fulfil God here on earth. At that time we were in the soul's world; our real existence was the soul. We said, "I am descending into the world only to please You, to fulfil You, to manifest You unconditionally." The people who you feel are very unjust have done something undivine, true. But look at your own promise. You expect perfection from other people; you feel that they have to do everything in a perfect way.

Perfection comes only when we fulfil our promise. Our first and foremost promise to God was to please Him and fulfil Him on earth. We have not fulfilled our promise; yet we expect others to fulfil their promise. We have done millions of things wrong and naturally, God is forgiving us. Otherwise, we would not be able to exist on earth. If He is ready to forgive us in spite of our countless defects and mistakes, how is it that we cannot forgive someone else?

My life is forgiven by God.
Therefore, my heart feels obliged
To forgive the world around me.

As spiritual seekers, we claim to be the chosen children of God. An unaspiring person who is wallowing in the pleasures of ignorance would never dare to claim God as his very own. But we dare to claim God as our very own, just because we have received an iota of God's good qualities. One of God's divine qualities is His Forgiveness.

If God forgives us twenty-four hours a day, can we not forgive someone else for one second? If our Source has the capacity to do something in infinite measure, naturally we also should have the capacity to forgive or illumine others who have done something wrong, according to our own standard.

Will you ever realise
That all your mistakes in life
Will be unmistakably followed
By God's Forgiveness?

CHAPTER TWELVE

God's Will

God's Will in an individual is progressive, like a muscle developing—strong, stronger, strongest. God's Will is to make an individual feel that there is something abiding, lasting, everlasting. When an individual reaches that stage, he will know God's Will. God's Will we can know from the sense of abiding satisfaction it gives us.

Anything that is eternal, anything that is immortal, anything that is divine, is God's Will. Even though God deals with Eternity, He is not indifferent for one second. For it is from one second, two seconds, three seconds that we enter into Infinity and Eternity. Let us try to feel God's Will in us at every second.

There is a very simple way to know what God's Will is for us as individuals. Every day when we start our day we build our own world. We make decisions. We feel that things have to be done in a certain way. I have to deal with this person in this way. I have to say this; I have to do this; I have to give this. Everything is I, I, I. If, instead of all this planning, we can make our minds absolutely calm and silent, we can know God's Will. This silence is not the silence of a dead body; it is the dynamic, progressive silence of receptivity. Through total silence and the ever-increasing receptivity of the mind, God's Will can be known.

When the human mind works powerfully, the divine Will cannot work. God's Will works only when the human mind does not work. When the mind becomes a pure vessel, the Supreme can pour into it His infinite Peace, Light and Bliss.

Right now we do not hear God's Voice. There may be something we hear from within that we feel is God's Voice, but it may be only a voice coming from our subtle physical or subtle vital or from somewhere else. But when we silence the mind, we can hear a silent voice inside the very depth of our heart or above our head, and that is the Voice of God. Once we hear the Voice of God, we cannot make any mistake in our life. If we listen to its dictates all the time, we will go forward, upward and inward constantly.

We are constantly building and breaking our mental house. But instead of making and breaking the house at our sweet will, if we can empty our mind, make it calm and quiet, then God can build His Temple or His Palace in us in His own way. And when He has built His Abode within us, He will say, "I have built this for you and Me to reside in together. I have built it, but it is not Mine alone. It is also yours. Come in."

The easiest way for us to know God's Will is to become the instrument and not the doer. If we become only the instrument for carrying out God's Plans, God's Will will act in and through us. God does the acting and He is the action. He is everything. We only observe.

> *To easily know what God's Will is,*
> *We have to feed the divine in us*
> *And illumine the human in us.*

How can I know God's Will in my daily life?

You can know God's Will in your daily life if early in the morning you offer your utmost gratitude to God for what He has already done for you. When you offer your gratitude-heart, then it expands; and when it expands it becomes one with God's Universal Reality. A gratitude-heart blossoms like a flower. When the flower is fully blossomed, then you appreciate and admire it.

In your case also, when your heart of gratitude blossoms, immediately God is pleased. If you offer gratitude to God for what He has already done for you, then naturally God's sweet Will will operate in and through you. Early in the morning, before you meditate or do anything else, offer as much gratitude as possible; offer your soulful tears just because you have become what you are now. If you do this, eventually you will become infinitely more than what you are now. Gratitude will be able to make you feel what God's Will is. God's Will will act in and through you and God will do everything in and through you, and for you, if you offer gratitude.

How can I know what God wants me to do?

You will know easily if you are not attached to the result or elevated by the result. Before you do something, pray to God: "God, if it is Your Will, then please inspire me to do it well." While working, tell God, "God, since I have accepted this work with the feeling that You wanted me to do it, please work in and through me so that I can do it well. From Your inspiration I will be able to know that it is Your Will." At the end of the work, whether the result comes as success or as failure, offer it at the Feet of God with the same joy.

How do I know if I am executing God's Will or I am fulfilling my own ego?

When you fulfil the demands of the ego, immediately you will feel that you are the lord of the world or that you are going to become the lord of the world. You are bloated with pride, and you feel that the rest of the world is at your feet. Once a desire of yours is fulfilled, immediately you feel, "Oh, my desire is fulfilled: I have become something, and the rest of the world will not achieve what I have." Always there will be a feeling of superiority when the ego is fulfilled.

When you execute the Will of God, the question of superiority or inferiority does not arise. At that time you feel only your oneness. You feel that God has appointed you or that God has accepted you as His chosen instrument, and that He is acting in and through you. No matter what you achieve, even if it is something very grand, extraordinary, unusual, you will not have any sense of personal pride. On the contrary, you will feel extremely grateful to God that He has chosen to fulfil Himself in and through you. There will be no pride, but only a feeling of expansion.

To execute God's Will means to achieve something. When you achieve something, you feel an expansion of your consciousness. But when you fulfil the demands of your ego, you feel totally separated from the rest of the world. You are the lord and the rest of creation is at your feet. In this way you can know the difference between the two.

Self-giving to God's Will
Is, without fail,
A slow-ripening
But most delicious fruit.

Should we pray for something we want or should we just pray for God's Will to be done?

To pray for God's Will to be done is the highest form of prayer. But a beginner finds it almost impossible to pray to God sincerely to fulfil him in God's own way. Early in the morning, a beginner will say to God, "God, I want to be Your unconditionally surrendered child." Then, the next moment, when jealousy, insecurity or pride enters into him, his self-offering becomes all conditional. At that time the seeker says, "God, early in the morning I prayed to You so sincerely to fulfil Your Will in me, but You did not listen to my prayer. Otherwise, I would have been above jealousy, fear, doubt, anxiety and attachment."

If the seeker prays for something in the morning and his prayer is not fulfilled in a few hours' time, immediately he becomes discouraged. Then he stops praying and meditating for six months. For a day he offers his sincere prayer, and then for six months he is ready to enjoy ignorance. So when a seeker is just starting out, it is always advisable for him to pray to God for whatever he feels he needs most, whether it is patience, purity, sincerity, humility or peace. Then God will give him peace, light and bliss, which are the precursors of something infinite that is going to come into his inner being.

Once he has received and achieved some peace, light and bliss and has become established to some extent in his inner being, he will have some confidence in God's operation and also in his own life of aspiration.

When one is making very fast progress or is a little advanced, he feels that there is a Reality within himself that is not going to disappoint or desert him. He feels that God is fully aware of what he needs and is eager to supply him with the things that he needs, because God wants to fulfil Himself in and through His chosen instrument. At His choice Hour, God will fulfil Himself in and through that particular chosen instrument.

When a seeker feels this kind of confidence within himself, that is the time for the seeker to pray, "Let Thy Will be done." At that time he can sincerely say, "God, now I want to please You only in Your own way." At that time he will feel that God wants to manifest Himself in and through him. He will feel that the moment God makes him perfect, he will be able to serve the divinity in humanity.

If a member of one's immediate family is sick, what is your feeling about praying to God for healing power?

Let us say that your mother is sick. Instead of saying, "Cure my mother, cure my mother," if you can say, "I place my mother at the Feet of God," you will be doing the best thing. Your best healing power will be to place your mother at the Feet of God, because He knows what is best.

When you offer your own will to the Will of God, you gain power, and this power will be utilised for God. God Himself will tell you how to utilise it. But if you try to heal on your own, in spite of your best intentions, you may stand against the Will of God.

Suppose you pray and meditate to acquire divine power so that you can cure people and help the world. You say, "I want to be a camel and carry the whole burden of the world on my shoulders." But if the camel is not illumined, then how can it help others gain illumination?

You are running toward your goal. If you ask God to give you something, then this is just an additional thing that you have to carry, and it may slow you down. If illumination is your goal, think only of your goal and nothing else.

Again, if a remedy for a disease comes spontaneously from within and you do not have to exercise your mental power or will-power, then there is no question of ego, pride or vanity. If in your meditation, all of a sudden you see inner light, and in this light you get a cure for some fatal disease, then naturally you will be able to offer this inner illumination to the world at large. But the best thing is to become illumined first. Then only will you be serving God in His own way. Otherwise at times you will serve God in His own way and at other times you will be feeding your own ego.

How can you tell the difference between the Will of God and wishful thinking?

In order to know God's Will, one need not be a great spiritual Master or a highly advanced soul. There are very few of these on earth, very few. But one has to be at least a seeker in order to know God's Will. How can one be a real seeker? One can be a true seeker if he feels that he is not only helpless, but also hopeless, meaningless and useless in every way without God. Without God he is nothing, but with God he is everything. He is aspiration. He is realisation. He is revelation. He is manifestation. If one has that kind of inner feeling about oneself, then one can be a true seeker overnight.

A sincere seeker tries to meditate devotedly each day. One who meditates devotedly each day will soon have a free access to God's inner Realm and be able to hear the Message of God. Of course, it is easy to say that you have to meditate devotedly, but to actually meditate devotedly may seem as difficult as climbing up Mount Everest. When you start meditating, you have to feel that your very life, your very existence, your very breath, is an offering to the Inner Pilot within you. Only in this way can you meditate devotedly and have a devoted feeling toward God.

During your meditation there comes a time when your mind is absolutely calm and quiet. There is only purity, serenity and profundity in your mind. Purity, sincerity and profundity have one common face, which is called tranquillity. When tranquillity is with them, they are perfect.

When the mind has become calm, quiet, tranquil and vacant, inside your heart you will feel a twinge, or you will feel something very tiny, like a soft bubble. It is a tiny thing, but there in golden letters is written a message. Even if you keep your eyes closed, no harm. Sometimes the message is transferred from the heart to the head, and with your mind you can see that the message has come. But if you have the capacity to go deep within, you will see that the message has already been inscribed in the heart. Just because you cannot see the message there, it has to come to the physical mind to convince you.

Inside the inmost recesses of the heart, where everything is flooded with purity, a message cannot be written by anybody other than God. There no undivine force can enter. This is not true about the mind. In the mind there can always be a mental hallucination, a fabrication or some self-imposed truth that we have created.

But in the inmost recesses of our heart, no disturbing thought, no struggling thought, no strangling thought will ever dare to enter. The depths of our heart are well protected, well shielded by God Himself, because God's own Wealth and Treasure is there. He Himself is there as a gatekeeper, guarding His Treasure.

When you meditate, please try to feel the necessity of opening your heart fully and closing your physical mind fully. The physical mind is the mind which thinks of your near and dear ones,

your friends, the rest of the world. When you bolt
the door of your physical mind and open the door
of your heart, the mind becomes calm and quiet
and the heart becomes all receptivity. When your
concentration and meditation are focused on the
heart and the heart is receptive, then naturally
what the heart treasures, the Message from God,
will come to the fore and you will be able to read
it and utilise it in your day-to-day life.

Now, it is one thing to hear the Message of
God correctly and another thing to listen to it and
fulfil it. There are quite a few who can hear God's
Message, but in their outer life they cannot execute it. For that, you need faith in yourself, faith
that you are not just a child of God, but a chosen
child of God. Everybody is God's child, but everybody cannot be God's chosen child because
everybody is not consciously aspiring. The chosen
are those who really want God here and now,
those who feel that they do not exist, cannot exist,
without God. Just because you aspire sincerely,
you can claim yourself as a chosen child of God.

When your aspiration-dedication-life
Is on earth
Only for the fulfilment of God's Will,
Then you are bound to feel
That your success-life
And progress-heart
Are nothing other than
An effortless effort.

How can I feel more positive about surrendering to God's Will?

When we surrender to God, we surrender to our highest part, for God is our most illumined part. We cannot separate God from our existence. If we feel that God and we are one, then God is our most illumined part, let us say, and we are right now unillumined. If we are wise and if we know that the One who is all-illumination is part and parcel of our existence, we will go there and receive from Him. If we take surrender in that way, then there is no problem.

But if we take surrender as the surrender of a slave to his master, then we will never be able to feel our oneness. The slave surrenders to his master out of fear. He is afraid that his service will be

144

dispensed with if he does not do his job well. He feels that no matter what he has done, even if he has done everything for the master soulfully, devotedly, even unconditionally, still there is no guarantee that the master will give him what he wants or that the master will really please him. If the master is an ordinary human being and if he has a few slaves, then he will get whatever he wants from his slaves; but when it is a matter of his own self-giving, he may be millions of miles away from their needs.

When we offer our existence to God, we have the feeling of oneness between Father and son or Mother and child. The little child always feels what his father has is his own. His father has a car. The child is only three years old, but he says, "I have a car." He does not have to say, "My father has a car." He will only say, "It is our car."

So if we change our understanding of our relationship with God, then there is no problem. If He has Peace, then we have every right to claim His Peace as our own. He is our Father, so we can inherit it. Because God is our Father, because God is our Mother, we can have that kind of feeling. If we feel that we are God's slaves and He is our Lord Supreme, that we are at His Feet and we have to do everything for Him, then we have no assurance, no guarantee that He will please us.

But if we have the feeling of oneness between father and son, between mother and child, then we will feel that what the mother or the father has, the child has every right to claim as his very own. A child does not surrender. He only legitimately claims his mother's wealth or his father's wealth as his very own.

We do not surrender anything; we only become aware of the fact that we belong to someone who has everything. We just go and claim it at any moment. For the feet to feel their oneness with the head is not at all difficult, because the feet know that the head also very often needs help from the feet.

Similarly, when we aspire, we come to feel that God needs us equally. As we need Him to realise the Highest, the Absolute Truth, so also He needs us for His manifestation. If it is not beneath God's dignity to take help from ignorant people for His manifestation on earth, then how can it be beneath our dignity to ask God to give us peace, light and bliss?

Once we establish our conscious oneness with God, there is no surrender. It is only mutual give and take. What the feet have to offer, the head takes gladly, and vice versa. We give God our aspiration and He gives us His Realisation. We give Him what we have, and He gives us what He has and is. In this way we do not surrender, we only claim each other as our very own.

Does developing our will-power interfere with our capacity to surrender?

If we have adamantine will-power, then we will get the capacity for unconditional surrender. Again, if we can surrender unconditionally, then we develop will-power. Inner will-power, which is the soul's light, and surrender, which is the heart's oneness with the Absolute, go together. There is no difference between the soul's will-power and unconditional surrender to the Will of the Supreme. Both of them are equally strong. If one can make unconditional surrender to the Will of the Supreme, it is the result of one's inner will-power, the soul's light.

Surrender your will to God's Will.
You will see that
All your disappointments
Will turn into unimaginable strengths.

How can we surrender to the Supreme?

It is very easy to surrender. You have already surrendered to ignorance. You cannot say that you have not surrendered to anybody. So you know the art of surrender. You can surrender to the Supreme in the same way that you have surrendered to ignorance. You have only to change your master. At every moment you have to feel the need of a new teacher. Somebody has taught you everything wrong; now the Supreme is waiting to teach you everything correctly. The one who has taught you is not the real teacher, but you have surrendered to him for hundreds and thousands of years. Now the same surrender you have to make to the Supreme.

If you refuse to surrender
To ignorance,
Then God will definitely allow you
To live inside
His Compassion-Harbour.

Each life has to become
A surrender-river
Before it can give what it has
And what it is
To the satisfaction-sea.

CHAPTER THIRTEEN

Fate versus Free Will

Fate is the result of the past. Free will is the result of the present. When we look backward, we feel the blow of fate. When we look forward, we see the dance of golden and energising free will.

The physical consciousness or the body-consciousness is limited. When we live in the body, we experience fate. The soul is ever-free. When we live in the soul, we experience free will. It is up to us whether we live in the body-consciousness or in the soul-consciousness.

The moment the soul enters into the body and we see the light of day, ignorance tries to envelop us, and fate starts its play. But light is not bound by fate. Light is the embodiment of free will. For our deplorable fate, we curse our forefathers, our friends, our neighbours, ourselves and finally God. But by cursing others, by cursing ourselves, we cannot solve our problems. We can solve our problems only if we know how to live the life of aspiration.

We are given ample opportunity to use our free will. It is we who have to utilise the opportunity in order to be fully, totally, unreservedly free. Very often seekers tell me, "Oh, I have a very unsatisfactory background." I tell them, "Why do you care for the past? The past is dust. But if you aspire, nobody can steal your present; nobody can steal your future. Your future can easily be golden."

Our free will is a child of God's infinite Will and at the same time it is part and parcel of God's infinite Will. We have only to allow it to break through the wall of ignorance and make us one with the Cosmic Will. Fate is the gate which leads us to the failure of the past. Free will is our acceptance of the future that wants to transform us, mould us, guide us and liberate us from fear, doubt, ignorance and death.

Do not surrender your will
To your deplorable fate!
Surrender your will
Only to God's all-loving,
All-protecting, all-illumining
And all-fulfilling Heart.

Is fate the same thing as karma?

There are three kinds of karma: *sanchita karma,*
prarabdha karma and *agami karma.* Sanchita
karma is the accumulation of acts from past lives
and this life whose results have not yet borne
fruit. In *prarabdha karma,* we are starting to reap
the fruit of some of the accumulated karma. If it
is bad karma, then we suffer. If it is good karma,
then we enjoy it. Finally comes *agami karma.*
When one is totally free from all ignorance, suffering and imperfection, when one has realised God
and is living only for the sake of God, at that time
one is enjoying the Free Will of the Supreme. This
is *agami karma.*

Most of us face *sanchita karma,* accumulated
karma which starts functioning as *prarabdha*
karma. There is no freedom, no free will, but only
fate all around us. It is like a devouring lion, striking from the past. But when we have *agami*
karma, this devouring lion becomes a roaring lion,
roaring for the divine Victory, the divine
fulfilment here on earth.

Do we truly reap all we sow, from every thought,
from every action?

As we sow, so we reap. This is true. But at the
same time, if you pray to God, if you meditate on

God, then God's Compassion can nullify the wrong forces that come from your bad thoughts. If you touch fire, naturally the fire will burn your fingers. At the same time, there will be some protective power to prevent you from touching the fire.

If a child goes and strikes another child, he knows that this child will come and strike him back. So what will he do? He will immediately go to his father. The father is stronger, and he protects the child. In this case, the Father is the Supreme. If you mix with ignorance and then ignorance wants to devour you, if you run to the Father before ignorance can devour you, the Father will show His utmost Compassion and save you from ignorance. It all depends on how much Compassion you can receive from the Supreme.

At what point does God's Compassion overrule the law of karma?

God's Compassion always overrules the law of karma. Had it been otherwise, no human being on earth could have lasted even for a single day. Again, from the highest spiritual point of view, you have to know that the law of karma does not mean severe punishment. It is a necessary experience for the seeker; it is the only way to accelerate his progress. Therefore, the law of karma itself is another form of God's Compassion. You may call it blessingful Love in disguise.

What is fate,
If not a limited reality?
A truth-seeker must always aim
At the unlimited Reality,
The infinite and immortal Supreme.

Is every event in our lives predestined, or is there just a general direction?

The most significant events in your life are predestined, but not what you are going to eat for breakfast. Again, even if it is predestined that you are going to die tomorrow, if you follow the spiritual life and God sees that you have genuine aspiration, you may not die. Instead, if it is God's Will, you may just have a headache. Fate can be changed by the Supreme's Will.

In the highest sense, the only thing that is predestined is that you are bound to realise God. Ignorance can prevent you from realising God today, but you cannot remain unrealised throughout Eternity. Let us use the term 'predestined' only in a good sense. If some calamity is going to take place, then you can use your will-power, your aspiration-power to change your fate. Fate can be changed by an unchanging will.

What is the role of man's free will?

Free will is our soul's consciousness-light. We can use the light of the soul for God-manifestation, or we may not use it at all. If we do not use it, then the aggressive part of the vital or the lethargy of the physical or the doubt of the mind comes into the picture and captures us. God does everything through the soul, which is His direct representative. God is the sun and the soul is like a lamp. This lamp embodies and represents the sun here on earth. But we usually do not remain in the soul's light and take full advantage of it, so our free will becomes our friendship with lethargy, our friendship with the doubting mind, our oneness with the heart's insecurity. Our free will either decides that the body, the vital and the mind have enough light to guide us, or it tells us that we are helpless without the guidance of our Lord Supreme.

How can we use our free will more?

As ordinary human beings, we have very limited free will. But if we become sincere seekers, then we will be surcharged eventually with an adamantine will. Now we are like a cow that is tied to a pole. There is a point beyond which we cannot go, but within these confines we have free will. The higher we go or the deeper we go in our meditation, the more our capacity increases.

When we can listen to the dictates of the soul, or when we can bring the soul forward to illumine our vital, our mind and our physical body, then our will becomes boundless. At that time, our individual will unites itself with the Universal Will within us. When the Universal Will becomes our will, at that time our freedom is infinite. Although we have free will to a very limited extent right now, this free will can be increased in infinite measure.

> *Where is your free will*
> *If you live inside*
> *Your binding mind?*
>
> *Where is your bondage*
> *If you live inside*
> *Your all-encompassing heart?*

Is my soul's will the same as God's Will?

Yes, God's Will and the soul's will are one and the same. But we have to know the difference between our soul's will and the urges of our demanding vital. Sometimes we take the pleasure-desires of the demanding vital as the soul's will. If we dive deep within, we are bound to know the real will of our soul, and that will and God's Will are inseparable. When that will is the seed that germinates and becomes a plant, we call it the soul's will. When it grows into a huge banyan tree, we call it God's Will. This Will eventually manifests itself in and through the soul, heart, mind, vital and body.

Are man's will and God's Will always in opposition?

To some extent it is true. Man can *unconsciously* stand against God's Will and, again, man can *consciously* stand against God's Will. Sometimes our conscience tells us what God's Will is, but we do not pay any attention to it. We feel that if we listen to the dictates of our conscience, then our ego will not be satisfied. Naturally, then we are standing against God's Will. Again, many times it happens that we are not diametrically opposing God's Will, but we do not know what God's Will is. At that time, we are not consciously standing against God's Will. We cannot say that at that time our will is in opposition to God's Will.

But we have to know that if we do not fulfil God's Will, either consciously or unconsciously, then we enter into ignorance and we delay our progress. A child may not know what fire can do to him. But if he touches fire, then the fire will burn him. I know that fire will burn me. But in spite of knowing this, I touch fire and I get burned. The result of unconscious opposition and conscious opposition is the same. But if somebody does it unconsciously, then he is helpless. In that case God's Grace descends sooner than otherwise.

If somebody knows the after-effects of his action, but in spite of that he does something wrong, then God's Grace will not come down immediately. The individual has to aspire again most sincerely and devotedly to bring down God's Grace from Above.

How can anything be outside the Will of the Supreme?

The Will of the Supreme is in everything, true. But we have to know what His ultimate Will is, and how much of that Will we are accepting as our own. He has given us a little limited freedom, just like the father who gives a penny to his child and watches to see how he uses it. If the child uses it for a good purpose, then the father gives him more—a nickel, then a dime.

God has given us limited freedom in order to examine whether we really want to do the right thing. We have to be very careful. His Will is inside us, so that when He gives us a penny we will be able to use it properly. But because we develop our own ego, individuality and personality, we try to use this penny in our own way instead of going deep within to see why He has given us the money. When He gives us something, immediately we want to squander it. But if we use it in His own way, then He gives us more and more.

God has given us freedom so that we will get joy. If He tells us, "I have given you a dollar. Now you have to use it for this or that purpose; I am giving it to you only for that," then we do not get joy. We feel that we are under compulsion. But when He says, "I have given you something. Now use it in your own way," then we misuse it. If we are wise, we will know that if we use it in His way, then He will give us much more.

On the one hand He is giving to us, and on the other hand, He is examining us. At the same time, inwardly He is inspiring us to do the right thing. But because we want to retain our individuality and personality, we try to use it in our own way. We use our own very limited will. What can poor God do? If we offer our will to His Will, only then are we safe, only then are we fulfilled.

Each time
I surrender myself cheerfully
To God's Will,
I see right in front of me
A free and fair highway
Leading to the Home
Of my Beloved Supreme.

CHAPTER FOURTEEN

The Meaning of Suffering

Suffering is an experience that God is having in and through us. It is the result of our limited consciousness. When unlimited consciousness operates, we see the result in the form of joy and delight. In the Infinite when we accomplish something, we are satisfied. But right now we are in the finite. When we accomplish something in the finite, we are not satisfied. When an individual has five dollars, he wants to make ten dollars. He suffers because he feels he is limited. Then when he makes ten dollars, he sees that somebody else has twenty dollars. Again, he suffers and enters into turmoil, thinking about how to make twenty dollars.

In the finite there will always be suffering because we try to compete, to grasp, to possess. But in the Infinite there is no suffering because once we enter into the Universal Consciousness, our will and the Universal Will are the same. Right now we are trying to satisfy the world with our limited consciousness, and the world also wants to satisfy us with its limited consciousness. We are limiting others and we ourselves are limited. Our main experience in this world is the experience of limitation, and that is why we suffer.

From the highest point of view, God embodies both the limited and the unlimited consciousness. He is the tiniest insect and at the same time He is the measureless cosmos. He is smaller than the smallest and larger than the largest. He is farther than the farthest and nearer than the nearest. He is nearer than the nearest for whom? For the seeker. He is farther than the farthest for whom? For the non-seeker.

For those who are wallowing in the pleasures of ignorance, God is farther than the farthest. Naturally those individuals suffer. But when a seeker prays to God and meditates on God, he feels that he is God's dearest child. When he prays to God he feels that God the Omniscient is there, listening to him. When he meditates on God he feels that God is talking to him and he is listening to God. If he is listening to God and God is listening to him, there can be no suffering.

If God is loving, why would He let us suffer?

Because of our wrong deeds, the negative, unaspiring, undivine forces have come into existence. When these forces enter into us, we suffer. Again, whatever we call suffering, and whatever we call sinful, evil, undivine or unaspiring, is also part of God. We experience God in and through everything. When we see suffering, immediately we feel that God is cruel. This is our human way of judging God. But if we go deep within, we see that what we call suffering is nothing but an experience. And who is having that experience? God Himself. God is the Doer, God is the action and God is the fruit.

If you suffer, thank God.
For nothing abides
Away from His Vision-Eye
And
His Compassion-Heart.

The human in us will see suffering as something horrible and undivine, but the divine in us will see it as God's experience in the process of cosmic evolution. The higher we go, the clearer it becomes to our human mind that all the incidents that have taken place on earth are the experiences of God in and through each human being. In God's Cosmic Game, we see multitudinous activities, countless forces operating all at once. But a day will dawn when the sincere seekers will realise the highest Truth and outnumber the unaspiring people, and then the undivine forces will have to give way.

When a seeker consciously enters into the sea of peace and light on the strength of his aspiration, he becomes part and parcel of God's Will. Then he does not commit the mistakes that unaspiring human beings commit. Unfortunately, right now, out of a million people, perhaps only one or two aspire; and again, out of those aspirants, a very limited few are extremely sincere in their spiritual life.

We have come to sing
The songs of joy
In this suffering world.

The world is progressing towards the Light, although this progress is very slow. Human suffering will come to an end, because God is all Delight. We come from Delight. On earth we are growing in Delight. At the end of our soul's journey we shall return to Delight. This experience of Delight we develop when we meditate and pray.

Most of us do not pray or meditate sincerely or soulfully; therefore, the existence of Delight is a far cry for us. But if we soulfully meditate and unconditionally surrender our day-to-day existence to the Almighty, to our Divine Father, then Delight will be our everyday reality. At every second we shall feel the presence of Delight. Our outer experience may be otherwise; it may seem painful or destructive. But in our inner experience we shall become inseparably one with the cosmic Will. In that Will there is no suffering. Suffering is in the human mind and in the earth-consciousness.

When we go beyond the earth-consciousness, when we offer our very existence to the Supreme and become part and parcel of His cosmic Will on earth, we see that there is no such thing as suffering. We see only an experience, a divine cosmic experience which God Himself is having in and through us.

Even in our heart's suffering-garden
Divinity's flower-fragrance-joy
Will eventually blossom.

Do pain and suffering aid our spiritual life somehow?

There is a general notion that if we go through suffering, tribulations and physical pain, then our system will be purified. This idea is not always founded upon reality. There are many people who are suffering because of their past karma or because undivine forces are attacking them, but we cannot say that they are nearing their destination. No! They have to aspire more sincerely in order to reach their destination.

We shall not welcome pain; we shall try to conquer pain if it appears. If we can take pain as an experience, then we can try to transform it into joy by our own identification with joy, which we then try to bring into the pain itself.

It is not necessary to go through suffering before we can enter into the Kingdom of Delight. Many people have realised God through love. The Father has love for the child and the child has love for the Father. This love takes us to our goal. Our philosophy emphasises the positive way of approaching Truth. We have limited light; now let us increase it. Let us progress from more light to abundant light to infinite Light.

Light, more light, abundant light,
Infinite light
We need every day
To illumine our ignorance-sufferings.

Can God eliminate the suffering in the world?

Yes, God can and does eliminate the suffering in the world. But who sincerely wants the elimination of suffering? We are all acting like camels. The camel eats cactus thorns until its mouth bleeds; then it goes and again eats thorns. In some way, consciously or unconsciously, the camel cherishes thorns. We human beings also cherish suffering, unconsciously or consciously. As long as we cherish suffering, suffering will remain on earth.

God really did not want
The human life
To be divided into
Half joy and half sorrow.

167

When we suffer unpleasant experiences and make mistakes, does that mean that the Supreme has withdrawn His Grace?

No, no, that is not true. It is just that ignorance-forces are there. If a child puts his finger into fire, that does not mean that the mother has less concern for the child. The mother has tremendous concern. But the mother is upstairs and the child has gone into the kitchen and placed his finger in the fire. Does that mean that the mother has no concern for the child? No. But the child is still ignorant. He does not know the power of fire.

When we do something wrong, at times it is because we do not know, and at times it is because we are tempted to do the thing. Sometimes the child knows that the fire will burn his finger, but he gets a kind of malicious pleasure in touching fire. With us also, in spite of knowing better, sometimes we enter into ignorance. It is like eating food. We know there is something called a sufficient quantity, but we overeat. We eat voraciously, and then we pay the penalty.

When we become, consciously or unconsciously, victims of temptation, we cannot say that God's Grace has withdrawn from our lives. Far from it! The mother can try to prevent the child from touching fire. She can say, "Do not do it, do not do it." But if the determination does not come from within, then when the divine forces try to prevent us from doing the wrong thing, we will feel a sense of loss. We will feel that we have missed something.

We have to feel that we are not losing anything by not entering into ignorance; or we have to feel that it is only a temporary necessity for us to make mistakes, because of our ignorance. If we live in light, there is no necessity to make mistakes. It is not because the divine Grace has been withdrawn that we become victims to ignorance. Far from it. But what can the divine Grace do? God has given us limited freedom. This limited freedom is like a knife. Somebody will use the knife to cut a mango and share it with others, and somebody else will use the knife to stab another person. Let us use the capacity that God has given us wisely.

If you are a true God-lover,
Then you will definitely feel
That your suffering-life
Is not desired by God.

Do accidents ever have a divine purpose?

If we look at an accident from the highest spiritual consciousness, then it is not an accident at all. It is just an incident, an experience that God is having in and through a particular human being. But in the outer world, in the field of manifestation, very often the wrong forces cause accidents. Sometimes the Supreme actually disapproves of these accidents. Sometimes He just tolerates them, and sometimes He approves of them. At the time of the accident the Supreme may feel that a particular person can be inspired to lead a better, more spiritual and more significant life. Someone may be disturbed by circumstances in his life, by members of the family, his neighbours and so forth, so that a new life can be opened to him.

If you look at it with your outer eyes, you may call it an accident. But you have to know, did God want that accident? Is it for the person's illumination? God never punishes us. He may give us an experience, but if we go deep within, we will feel that it is God who is actually having this experience. If we can identify ourselves consciously with the Will of the Supreme, then there is no such thing as an accident.

If suffering comes to us, what can we do?

We have to make the best of it. We have to take it as something unavoidable or as a blessing. It is a blessing in the sense that we can derive some advantage or some benefit from it. The benefit we derive is that we will not repeat the same error, we will not commit the same mistake again and again.

If we are suffering, we have to be conscious of the mistake we have made. When we become conscious of our mistake, automatically a sense of purification dawns in us. But in order to achieve purity, we do not have to go through suffering. No! For God-realisation, suffering is not necessary. What is needed is love of Truth, love of Light. If we allow light to enter into us and remain inside us, then there will not be any suffering.

Why do you have to think
Of your difficulties
As negative forces?
Just think of them
As opportunities.
Lo, they will increase
Your inner and outer capacities!

CHAPTER FIFTEEN

Immortality and Eternity

Immortality deals with life, life in the form of consciousness, life in the form of reality and life in the form of object, subject or substance. Immortality means the immortality of consciousness, not the immortality of the gross physical. One can leave the body at one's own sweet will. But if anything has to last on the physical plane for an indefinite time, it becomes the greatest torture. Even the most materialistic person on earth, even a pleasure-loving person, will be disgusted if he stays on earth for more than one hundred years. Every undivine desire may be fulfilled, but even then he will be disgusted because he is not dealing with the illumining consciousness.

When you deal with the illumining consciousness, you do not pay attention to the senses. You feel that you do not need the satisfaction of the senses, or of anything that belongs to earth, because at that time you see that earth itself is impermanent. The only thing that is permanent is the birthless and deathless Divine.

When we think of Eternity, we have to know that anything that is created, whether on the physical plane, the vital plane, the mental plane or the transcendental plane, can be eternal. It may have had its beginning yesterday, but it can go on, go on for millions and billions and trillions of years.

Immortality deals with life, and life came from Silence. We can measure Eternity, but we cannot measure Immortality. However, Immortality came first, because Silence itself was life. So life comes first, and then only can we start measuring. First one is born, then one is one second old, one day old, one year old, and so on.

So in Eternity there is a sense of measurement, while there is none in Immortality. You cannot measure Immortality, whereas you can try to calculate Eternity with your imagination. The sense of measurement comes in Eternity. It is divine, intuitive and psychic measurement. Immortality is something that is already there.

Let us take Eternity as a tree that is growing, growing and growing. Eternity grows and Immortality remains the same. Immortality is already there; just use your vision. But Eternity is always going upwards. Eternity's conception goes upwards, while Immortality is all around.

173

Do not waste your time
Thinking of Eternity.
Do immediately
What you are supposed to do.
Since Eternity exists,
It will definitely bring you the reward
For your today's self-giving.

Does God plan for the future the way human beings do?

God's Vision is not something to be fulfilled in the future. God is omnipotent, omniscient and omnipresent. God's perception and manifestation are simultaneous.

Man, being God's instrument, plans; and later he sees the unfoldment of his plans in time. However, God's Play is more like a child's play in that it is spontaneous and without motive, and it does not seek a future result. God is a divine Child but His Play, unlike that of a human child, is responsible, conscious and divine.

It is good for man to have a plan. God manifests Himself through man. With our finite consciousness, Truth is revealed gradually as ignorance melts into Light. But in God's world, Truth and Revelation exist together, so that perception and manifestation occur simultaneously. For man the vision of the future must be fulfilled through plans so that God may reveal through man what has always abided in Him.

Do you think that God lives
All by Himself?
No, He lives with millions
Of secret and sacred plans
For you.

How can we best utilise the physical earthbound time that we are living in?

There are two kinds of time. One is earthbound time and the other is eternal Time. The earthbound time is what we have created, but eternal Time cannot be created. It is within us and without us.

When we live in eternal Time, we cannot separate one second from another second. When we live in earthbound time, we know that it is one o'clock and then it is one minute past one. They are two separate minutes. But in eternal Time, we cannot separate the minutes or hours. In eternal Time one o'clock, two o'clock, three and four o'clock are all together. This is the difference between eternal Time and earthbound time. We can see the present, past and future perfectly housed in eternal Time, and this eternal Time we can easily possess when we are Self-realised.

Let us take an ordinary second. This second you can use either for meditation or for gossip. This second you can use either to pray or to cherish impure and undivine thoughts. When you consciously use time to do something divine, you are entering into divine Time, which means timeless Time. When you are consciously thinking of something divine, immediately eternal Life comes and shakes hands with you. Each moment you want to go upward through aspiration, the eternal Time also becomes your friend.

Love God unconditionally!
You will not be chained
By earthbound time.

Many say that we are entering into the end of this age, and that the world is going to end quite soon. I was wondering what you had to say about it.

Since your childhood I am sure you have been hearing that the world is coming to an end. Our grandfathers were also told the same story. The world is not just a tiny spot. It will not be destroyed totally. A portion of the world may be destroyed by an earthquake or some catastrophe, but the whole world as such is not going to be destroyed. Human aspiration is not going to come to an end.

Human aspiration may ascend and descend, but ultimately it goes up. If somebody becomes tired while he is climbing, then in his time of relaxation perhaps he may come down a little. But when he is again inspired, he will go up again and finally he will reach the Highest.

The world is not going to come to an end, because human aspiration is not going to come to an end. One day human aspiration may be very hot, and another day it may be lukewarm, but once it starts in us, it will carry us to the highest Absolute. Before it reaches that Goal, it will not be satisfied. As long as human aspiration exists in the earth atmosphere, this world will never be totally destroyed.

Aspire soulfully and sleeplessly.
You will see that
The death-dealing hand of time
Will be transformed into
The life-flowing heart of time.

His mind-clock tells him
That he does not have to waste
His precious time
Waiting for God,
Since God's existence is quite uncertain.

His heart-clock tells him
To wait and watch,
For God will definitely come.

His soul-clock tells him
That God has already arrived
And asks him what he is doing
And why he is not taking care
Of the Supreme Guest.

CHAPTER SIXTEEN

Religion and Spirituality

God is one, but at the same time He is many. A tree is one, but it has so many branches. When you look at a branch, you feel it is the tree. When you look at the leaf, you feel it is the tree. Similarly, God may be seen differently from different angles. But He is the same God. All religions are part of one God-Tree. This God-Tree has many branches, flowers and fruits. If you climb up a tree and rest on a particular branch, will the tree be displeased? Similarly, if you take a flower or fruit, no matter from which branch, the God-Tree will be pleased, for each branch is part and parcel of the Tree itself.

Is there any real difference between one religion and another?

There is no fundamental difference between one religion and another, because each religion embodies the ultimate Truth. Each religion is right, absolutely right, because each religion conveys the message of Truth in its own way. There is only one Truth, but it is called different names by different people. Your religion may say one thing, and my religion may say something else. But our religions will never differ when it is a matter of the highest Truth.

The ultimate Goal of every religion is to realise the highest Truth. On the way to our Goal, we may misunderstand each other. Why? Precisely because there are many roads that lead to the Goal. Some will follow one road and some will follow another road. Each road will be able to offer inspiration. One person will say that his road is by far the best because it is pleasing him. Another person will say that his road is the best. But when both reach their destination, they will be at the same Goal: Truth. In Truth there is no conflict; Truth or God-realisation transcends all religions.

God has made many roads
Leading to Him
Since God wants to please
Each individual in his own way,
As He Himself wants to be pleased
In His own way.

What are the qualities of a true religion?

There are two kinds of religion: false religion and true religion. False religion wants to change the face of the world by any means, even by foul means—by hook or by crook. True religion wants only to love soulfully the heart of the world. True religion has a universal quality. It does not find fault with other religions. A false religion will say that it is the only valid religion and its prophet is the only saviour. A true religion will feel that all prophets are saviours of mankind.

A false religion tries to exercise its Himalayan supremacy over other religions. A true religion only sympathises with other religions. It wants to experience its oneness-ecstasy with all religions, founded upon its own soulful cry. It wants to become inseparably one with all religions by virtue of its tolerance, patience, kindness and forgiveness. Forgiveness, compassion, tolerance, brotherhood and the feeling of oneness are the signs of a true religion. Again, a true religion knows perfectly well that it is the Supreme Pilot Himself who is loving and piloting each religion, and at the same time forgiving the weaknesses and shortcomings that each religion unfortunately embodies.

A true religion is one that, down the sweep of centuries, will love mankind with all its imperfections. And on the strength of its oneness-love it will try to bring about a new world—not by force, not by lording it over others, but by becoming inseparably one with others.

A true religion has the capacity to show its followers the invisible truth. A true religion has the capacity to make its followers feel the incredible Love divine. A true religion has the capacity to grant its followers the seemingly impossible reality: perfection within and without.

Aren't all religions really worshipping the same God?

There is one absolute Supreme. All religious faiths worship the same God, but they address Him differently. A man will be called 'Father' by one person, 'Brother' by another and 'Uncle' by another. When he goes to his office, he is called by his surname. When he mixes with his friends, they will call him by his given name. He is the same person, but he is addressed in different ways, according to one's connection with him. Similarly, God is addressed in various ways, according to one's sweetest, most affectionate feeling.

What is your opinion of those religious sects which fight with other sects in the Name of God?

I feel very sad when religious sects quarrel and fight in the Name of God. If they really love God, they will not kill others in His Name. Love means oneness. If we have oneness, how can we fight? We fight only because we do not feel love for others, because we have not yet transformed our ignorance into oneness-reality.

In our own being there are many members—the body, vital, mind, heart and soul—and we claim all of them as our own, very own. The body, too, has so many parts, but when we want to achieve something, all the parts work together. In exactly the same way, when we want to do something good for mankind, then all the religions can and should work together.

Since we all have the same Source, we all have the same ultimate destination. Since "all roads lead to Rome," and we are all heading ultimately to the same Source, it is ridiculous to fight against others who are following different roads. Some people may choose a very short and direct road, while others may take a longer route. Some may want to fly, while others are content to walk.

When all religions work together, they can achieve something great and good for both God and humanity. It is the collective prayers and good will of the followers of all the world's religions that will bring down the highest Love and Compassion from Above. And it is only God's Love and Compassion descending into humanity's heart and life that can change the face and fate of the world.

How can religion overcome a narrow outlook and develop a real acceptance of all other religions as true and necessary?

Religion as such cannot overcome this narrow outlook. Only when religion takes help from spirituality, its elder brother, does it become possible to overcome this narrow outlook. Religion sees God, but spirituality makes the seeker become God. Religion can go as far as believing in the Light or even seeing the Light. But spirituality goes much higher, much deeper. It helps the seeker grow into the Light itself and become one with God-Consciousness and God-Light.

Religion stops at seeing the reality; it does not want to grow into reality. Spirituality, like religion, sees what the reality is, but then it goes one step ahead and wants to consciously grow into the reality itself. So if religion takes help from spirituality, then it is quite possible to overcome all the narrow outlooks found in religion.

Spirituality is not merely tolerance. It is not even acceptance. It is the feeling of universal oneness. In our spiritual life, we look upon the Divine not only in terms of our own God, but in terms of everybody else's God. Our spiritual life firmly and securely establishes the basis of unity in diversity. Spirituality is not hospitality to another's faith in God. It is the absolute recognition of the other's faith in God as one's own.

Religion says,
"If you accept me in my way,
Then you are good."
Spirituality says,
"You do not have to follow my way.
Follow your own way soulfully
And reach your destined goal."

What does God like best in a religion?

What God likes best in each religion is a oneness-heart. First let each religion tolerate the others. Once tolerance is there, then let each religion go one step further. Let it recognise other religions also. Once recognition is given, each religion has to sincerely feel that other religions are as good as it is. It has to feel that each religion is right in its own way, that all are equal.

Tolerance of others exists only as long as there is a sense of separativity. Once a particular religion gives due value to other religions and sees their existence as an expression of Truth, then that particular religion can go high, higher, highest and deep, deeper, deepest. Seeing and establishing its conscious oneness with all other religions, it can claim that there is only one religion. When a religion comes to realise that all religions form one eternal religion, one eternal eye of Truth, one eternal heart of Truth, then that religion is perfect. This kind of discovery and achievement God likes best in all the world religions.

When I speak to you about God,
You don't believe me.
When you speak to me about God,
I don't believe you.
Therefore, what is the use
Of our talking to each other
About God?
The best thing will be for us
To pray for God to speak,
For He is the only One
Who can talk about Himself
With inner Illumination
And outer Compassion.

What is the role of religion in the process of God-realisation?

Each religion is like a house. In the beginning, you have to live in a house; you cannot live in the street. But a time comes when your consciousness expands and the whole world becomes your house. At that time you cannot be bound by the limitations of any one particular house. You accept all religions and, at the same time, you go beyond the domain of religion and achieve conscious oneness with God.

187

Each religion is like a river. When the river enters into the God-realisation-ocean, it has played its part. At that time, the river becomes the ocean itself; it has become one with the Source.

If you follow a religion, you are on the road to your destination. But if you want to reach the ultimate Truth, then you have to concentrate, meditate and contemplate. That does not mean that you will not go to your church or synagogue anymore. But if you feel an inner call deep within your heart to run fast, faster, fastest towards your Goal, then you have to practise the inner life, the life of self-discipline and meditation.

Religion will tell us there is a God. It will tell us that we have to be good, we have to be kind, we have to be simple, sincere and pure. But spirituality will say that it is not enough just to know that God exists. We also have to see Him, we have to feel Him, we have to grow into Him. This we do through prayer and meditation.

CHAPTER SEVENTEEN

Heaven and Hell

Heaven and hell are largely in our mind. If you treasure a good thought, then you are creating Heaven. If you cry to God for light, then you get a good experience, an illumining experience, and this experience is nothing but Heaven. Again, if you treasure a negative thought, then you are creating hell. Heaven and hell can be experienced every day.

When the mind becomes a victim to worries, anxieties and other undivine forces, when the mind is disturbed, agitated, tortured by ugly, impure and undivine thoughts, we feel that we are in hell. But when the beauty, light and divinity of the heart come to the fore and we try to reveal and manifest them in the aspiring world, then we feel that we are in Heaven.

We do not have to wait for death to find hell or Heaven. Both of them are within us in our daily life, in our daily conduct. If we are always soulful and surrendered, we are in a position to remain always in Heaven in this very life on earth.

Each time I enjoy a pure thought,
I feel that I am living
In my own homemade Heaven.

Just because we have not yet experienced the Infinite, the Immortal and the Eternal, we feel that the opposite—the finite—is hell. But the bondage that we are experiencing every day is only a passing phase. It is like an overcast day. For a few hours the sun may not shine, but finally the sun comes out. Each individual has an inner sun. This inner sun is now covered by fear, doubt, worries, anxieties, imperfections and limitations. But a day will come when we will be able to remove these clouds and then the inner sun will shine brightly.

If we believe in hell, then we are only belittling our own inner potentiality. We are all God's children. For us there is no hell; there is only light. But if we do not see the truth in the way that the truth has to be seen, then there is inner pain. This pain is bound to occur every day in our life. The truth is there, but we have to see the truth in the proper way. Then only will we see that life has its true meaning.

To find Heaven on earth
Is not a difficult task.
Your gratitude-heart can show you
Where Heaven is.

Every day we can have a sense of Heaven. Heaven means infinite peace, light and bliss. When a seeker prays and meditates, he enters into Heaven. When his mind is calm and quiet, when his mind is tranquillity's flood, his heart becomes all-giving and his life becomes Divinity's Reality. Heaven is not a place; it is a state of consciousness. When we free our mind from the meshes of ignorance, when we liberate our existence from the mire of earth, we see, feel and grow into Heaven.

Beauty upon beauty
Descends from Heaven
When my heart becomes the receptivity
Of luminescent stillness.

What is the spiritual value of the earth?

Those who accept life, those who accept Mother-Earth as something real, feel that they have a bounden duty to perform here. This duty is nothing other than conscious realisation of God. Unconscious awareness of God everybody has. If one is not an atheist, if one does believe in God, then he will have awareness or at least unconscious awareness of God. But a seeker becomes consciously aware of God's Presence. He meditates on God and gradually, gradually, his own consciousness develops to such an extent that he feels God's Presence constantly, everywhere. He feels that it is his bounden duty to reveal God's Presence, which he feels and which he sees with his own heart and his own eyes. Finally, he feels that he has to manifest his realisation of the highest Truth. Realisation and manifestation of the ultimate Truth have to take place here on earth, and nowhere else.

A sincere seeker is a divine hero. He fights against teeming darkness to fulfil God's Will here on earth. Otherwise there will always be a yawning gulf between earth and Heaven. This earth of ours must be transformed into Heaven, into a place of joy, peace, bliss and delight.

Be ready to fly, my body.
You will enjoy flying
Like your big brother, soul,
In the silence-vision of Heaven.

Be ready to walk, my soul.
You will enjoy walking
Like your little brother, body,
In the sound-reality of earth.

When you say that earth can easily be transformed into Heaven, do you mean physically as well?

You have to know what we mean by Heaven. Heaven does not mean a place with big houses, big palaces or estates. No! Heaven is in our mind. When we enjoy divine thoughts, we are in Heaven. When we cherish undivine thoughts, we are in hell. Heaven and hell are states of consciousness.

What each human being has is consciousness. It is through consciousness that we see reality. When we aspire, our finite consciousness becomes infinite. This is Heaven. It is certainly true that we will all have a divine life, but that does not necessarily mean a physically immortal life. The consciousness of Heaven is immortal. But if we feel that the physical will remain immortal, as Heaven is immortal, we are mistaken. This physical body will live for sixty, eighty, one hundred, perhaps even two hundred years and then go.

The very conception of Heaven is something bright, luminous, delightful and, at the same time, immortal. But we have to know what is immortal in us. It is the aspiring consciousness in us. When we say that earth will be transformed into Heaven, that means that anything that is within us or in the world which is now imperfect, obscure or unaspiring will be transformed eventually into perfection.

Where is the marriage
Of Heaven and hell?

The marriage of Heaven and hell
Is in the mind's dry desert
And in the heart's loving nest.

CHAPTER EIGHTEEN

Good and Evil

In the beginning there was only Silence and infinite Light. Then each individual was given a limited amount of freedom, but we misused that limited freedom to such an extent that we created, in some ways, our own world of ignorance, inconscience and undivine forces. We are like a cow tied to a tree with a rope. While using the little freedom that it has, the cow runs around and destroys everything in reach.

Evil is in our mind, not inside our aspiring heart. The mind wants to taste the whole world infinitesimally, piece by piece. The heart wants to embrace the whole world as a unit. The heart feels that the whole world belongs to it. The mind says, "This is mine. That is yours." The more the mind can separate, the greater joy the mind gets. Evil is a sense of separativity. When there is union, there is no evil. If we have good will, love, a feeling of oneness, then instead of destroying the world, we shall try to embrace the whole world.

It is the same old story: disobedience. If we obey the inner law, then nothing happens. But when we disobey the inner law, evil comes into existence. If we properly use our freedom, then we go towards the Divine, towards the Light. But if we misuse it, then we become anti-divine; we become a hostile force.

It was not God's intention that there should be undivine forces. But many things happen in this world that are tolerated. It is one thing for something to be fully sanctioned and another thing for it to be just accepted or tolerated. If parents have bad children, what do they do? Disobedient, naughty children they just tolerate. We are all God's children. Some are good, some are bad. But God did not intend to have a bad creation.

God is omnipresent. He is in good and He is also in so-called evil. If a tiger wants to devour me, I feel that the tiger is an undivine force. But God's existence is also inside the tiger. Everything is in the process of evolution toward greater God-manifestation. No matter what stage of evolution a person or thing has reached, God is still inside that person or thing.

Right now I am drinking distilled water. It is good water. But water can also be dirty, filthy, impure. God can be found inside impure water as well as inside pure water. But even though God is there, I will not drink impure water because I know it will harm my body.

Spiritual people who are meditating are trying to see God at a particular level of consciousness. God is in bad things also, but we do not want to go back to the animal kingdom and the lower realms of consciousness to look for God.

Are you saying that God is not wholly good, that He is both good and evil?

Yes. God is in both good and evil and, again, He is above them both. It is like a tree. Let us say the roots are evil and the branches are good. But they are one; they are part of the same tree. Evil is a lower manifestation of Truth and good is a higher manifestation of Truth. There is no night without light; even in the blackest night there is always at least an iota of light. But God is in both of these and above them both, as the sky is above the tree.

If you say God is not in evil, then you are saying that God is not omnipresent. And that is like saying that God is not God. God is in both, but He is not bound by them. He is like a boat which is in the water and also above the water.

From the strictly spiritual point of view, there is no such thing as good or evil. Evil only exists in the mental world. What we think of as being evil is actually lesser truth or imperfection growing into greater truth or more perfect reality.

> *When I dive deep within,*
> *I see no imperfection-jungle*
> *Or even difficulty-fern,*
> *But only the smile of perfection*
> *And the dance of satisfaction-delight.*

I cannot understand how anything created by God can be imperfect. How can He create a soul that is not perfect at the beginning and then say, "All right, you go ahead in your own way; develop as best you can"?

God does not throw the soul heartlessly into the manifestation. The soul is not alone. God Himself is always inside the soul. We have come from God and we are a part of Him. But where is our realisation? Where is our perfection? We are in the process of consciously attaining this realisation and perfection. Each individual represents God, but each individual has not consciously realised Him.

The Absolute God, who is the Supreme Self, is perfect. The Highest, the One without a second, the God who created the multiplicity, is always perfect. But the God who has entered into the earth-plane for evolution has accepted imperfection because He has taken on the earthly consciousness, which is full of limitations and imperfections.

Do you believe in sin?

What others call 'sin', I call 'imperfection'. We have been created by God, who is all Love, all Delight. When we can remove the veil of ignorance from our consciousness, we will immediately enter into the world of perfection. There, there is no such thing as sin. Sin is in our mind; it can never be in our soul. What is sin? It is something that binds and restricts, like a prison-cell. And what is delight? It is the boundless freedom of perfection.

From the philosophical point of view, what some people call evil or sin, we think of as ignorance— the constant play of Maya or illusion. He who is caught in this play is different from the liberated soul who is freed from this illusion of reality. It is by meditation that we can free ourselves from ignorance, from illusion, and transform our human nature into divine nature.

> *Your heart's cheerful willingness*
> *To obey God*
> *Will wash away*
> *Your mind's ignorance*
> *Of millennia.*

What do you mean by ignorance?

The definition of ignorance in one short sentence is limited consciousness. When we enter into unlimited consciousness, ignorance disappears.

In this world there is light, more light, abundant light, boundless light and infinite Light. If we take ignorance as destruction, then we are mistaken. We have to see that what we call ignorance consists of limited light. Even in the darkest night there is some light. Otherwise, we could not exist at all. A child, in comparison to his elder brother, naturally is ignorant; but the child also has some light in him.

So what we call ignorance is light in a different form. I as an individual, you as an individual and she as an individual have limited light—let us say infinitesimal light—compared to God, who is infinite Light. But through our prayer and meditation, we are growing into God's boundless and infinite Light and becoming all that God has and all that God is.

What we call ignorance is nothing short of an experience which God is having in and through us. If we become conscious of the fact that we are only His instruments, then we are not bound by ignorance. We see that there is someone, the Inner Pilot, who is playing His Cosmic Game in and through us. If we know that we are mere instruments, then there is no ignorance, there is no light; there is only the Supreme, who is everything. He is the Doer, He is the action, He is the result; He is everything. But if we feel or think that we are doing everything, we are making a Himalayan mistake.

There shall come a time
When each and every human being
Will be flooded with the soul-courage
To silence the pride of ignorance-night.

You speak of night and light. Do you believe that parts of life are dark and imperfect?

Life is composed of perfection, but we can say that there is lesser perfection and greater perfection. We cannot say that this side is black and that side is white; we will say that on this side there is comparatively less light. So there is no negative and positive; there is only positive. But the thing that is less positive has less capacity, and sometimes we call it negative.

I once read that if you choose evil, you are not really free. I thought it was an interesting idea. Would you enlighten me?

First of all we have to know what evil is. Anything that limits us, anything that binds us, is evil. Evil will come to us in the form of pleasure, and when we surrender to the pleasure that evil brings, we are caught. The evil that wants to make us its instrument for its own purpose makes us feel that we are helpless and ignorant, and that is the reason we accept it.

Sometimes we may have no freedom in our outer life, but in our inner life we have a considerable amount of freedom. We can pray, we can concentrate, we can meditate even in a prison cell. But when evil possesses us, our inner freedom goes away, and our outer freedom also deserts us. At that time we are bound to seek the fulfilment of our desires or evil impulses.

Everything has a nature of its own. The very nature of evil is to bind; the very nature of divinity is to liberate. The nature of scorpions is to sting. We cannot expect them to behave differently. Therefore, we must not give them the opportunity to sting us. We have to stay away from them at all times. If we stand in front of a scorpion to exert our own freedom, it is foolishness. We have to feel the necessity of staying only with something which constantly liberates and illumines us, and that is light.

How can we prevent the wrong forces from operating in our lives or in the lives of our dear ones?

There are two sensible ways. The first way is through concentration, meditation and contemplation. If one knows how to do these well, then he need not enter into the world of wrong forces. During your soulful meditation, you can ask God for solid strength, spiritual strength. If you can apply this solid strength in your life, then the bad forces are bound to disappear from your life.

The second way is to try to see the ultimate Truth, God, in everything. This we have to do with our soul's light. Each human being has a soul. The soul is an infinitesimal portion of the infinite Truth. The soul is in direct contact with the Divine, with the Transcendental Being. The problem is that when we speak to a person, we do not approach his soul. We see only the outer body. The physical is full of darkness and imperfections, so it is difficult for us to approach the soul. But let us try to see the soul inside the physical being of the person and commune with the soul and bring to the fore the soul's light.

When we achieve complete oneness with God, do we still see a polarity between good and evil?

When we are in a state of oneness with God, we cannot say that this is evil and that is good. When we become one with God, everything is a manifestation of the divine Will. But when we are not one with God, then one second we are with God, in God, and for the next hour we are in ourselves—in our own vital, in our own physical consciousness. Then there will always be both undivine and divine forces within and around us. But when we have the highest, most sublime meditation, we do not see the polarities of good and evil. For then we are one with the Transcendental Reality, and this transcends all human notions of good and evil, divine and undivine.

Faith can believe everything
That we say.
Belief can increase
The strength of faith.
Belief is pure.
Faith is sure.
Belief looks around
To see the Truth.
Faith looks within
Not only to feel the Truth
But also to become the Truth.

CHAPTER NINETEEN

Faith in God

The life of a seeker is the life of inner faith. Faith is something that constantly brings us the message of the Beyond. Faith is the foundation of our real life. We must have faith in God; we must have faith in ourselves. If we have faith only in God and not in ourselves, or if we have faith in ourselves and not in God, then we cannot go very far.

What is our faith? Our faith is our inner cry for God's Light and Bliss in infinite measure. Our faith is God's transcendental Smile, which transforms our life and carries us from the sea of ignorance to the sea of wisdom. Our inner faith in God constantly helps us to run the fastest and constantly makes God run toward us in the fastest possible way. Because God's speed is far greater than our speed, when we take one step toward God we see that God has taken ninety-nine steps toward us. Then we meet together.

Our faith in God is very often conditional; but God's faith in us is always unconditional. We start our spiritual journey with fifty percent faith, saying, "God, I shall give You this; then You can give me that. I shall give You my aspiration; then You will give me Your Blessings."

Faith is the eye that sees the future in the immediacy of the present. If we have faith in the spiritual life, we do not stumble, we do not walk, we do not march. No! We simply run the fastest. If we have implicit faith in God, if we have implicit faith in the Inner Pilot and in our own aspiration, then we constantly run the fastest towards our destined goal.

Our faith in God
Prescribes solutions
To each and every problem
That our mind creates.

We have to have faith that we can realise God, either in this incarnation or in some future incarnation. We have to have faith that we can be the possessor of infinite Light, Peace and Bliss. We have to have faith in our aspiration, in our concentration, in our meditation and contemplation. Then only will the goal of God-realisation and the divinisation of human nature and earth-consciousness become ours.

I feel that I am a child of God and I also feel, unfortunately, that I am a child of belief, tradition and all sorts of things. Is it possible to be free from all past beliefs and be absolutely one with God?

Through sincere aspiration you can get rid of the mental beliefs or worldly beliefs that you have kept in your heart and mind. You can replace them with your soul's spontaneous light, which expresses itself as inevitability or immediate assurance. This feeling of inevitability and assurance, which is based on the soul's light, can be established in your mind and heart. Then the so-called worldly beliefs you can discard as you discard old clothes.

It is not only possible but inevitable; in fact it is necessary for God-realisation. Otherwise, these old beliefs in the form of society's dictates or in the form of traditional morality will hamper your spiritual progress.

In human belief there is always a mixture of doubt. Fifty percent will be belief, fifty percent will be doubt; or one percent may be belief and as much as ninety-nine percent may be doubt. But when you live in the soul and are illumined by the soul's light, you will get assurance not only from the soul but also from the soul's inevitability, which is absolutely one with God's dynamic Reality and God's dynamic Vision. At that time you can go beyond all beliefs and be in direct, constant oneness with God, the highest Reality.

When you live in the soul constantly and express its highest Truth, old beliefs will have no place in your life.

Your mind may be chained
To doubt,
But your heart is always hoisting
Faith's victory-banner.

What do you think of a person who is an atheist?

We say that someone is an atheist because he says that there is no God. When he goes to that extreme, he will see that his negative feeling itself is a form of positive feeling. At the extreme he says that there is nothing. But what he calls nothing is, for us, something; and that very thing we call God.

Sometimes the sky is overcast with clouds and there are no stars or moon visible. We know that when these clouds are dispersed, we will immediately be able to see the moon and the stars. But an atheist cannot see beyond the clouds, and he stays with the clouds.

Does faith help us to raise our consciousness?

Every day we are assailed by doubt, and every day we are inspired and energised by faith. When we are assailed by doubt, what we notice is our conscious fall. We cannot expand; we doubt our own capacity, even our very existence. When doubt enters into our mind early in the morning, it is impossible for us to come out of our tiny mental room. But when we are inspired and energised by faith, we feel that the whole world belongs to us.

Each human being has both doubt and faith. The moment he uses his doubt-instrument, he feels that everything in his life is circumscribed. His progress comes to a standstill. But when he uses the other instrument, faith, he feels that he is flying up to the highest plane of consciousness and singing the song of the ever-transcending Beyond.

Every day we can bind ourselves or we can free ourselves. We sing the song of bondage consciously or unconsciously by feeding the teeming doubt within us. We fall from the reality-tree again and again when we play with our doubt-friend. But when we dive deep within and bring our heart-illumining and soul-manifesting faith to the fore, we climb up the reality-tree high, higher, highest.

Your question is:
How far can faith take you?
My answer is:
As far as you want,
To see God-Eternity's
Infinity-Smile.

We have to be faithful both in the inner world and in the outer world. When we are faithful to our inner and outer life, we feel that our divinity is blossoming petal by petal. When we go deep within, we see that there is only one person who is constantly and eternally faithful to us, and that is God. From time immemorial He has been faithful to us, faithful to His creation.

If we follow the spiritual life, naturally we will want to go to the Source, which is God. We will want to be as divine and great as the Source. If our ultimate aim is to become divine or to become God Himself, then we have to be faithful to the world that we are living in. We have to attend at every moment to what we say and what we think. When a thought comes to us, if it is a divine thought, then we have to feel that it is a blessing that has entered into us. This blessing we have to offer to the world around us. If we can faithfully and silently offer this divine thought to the outer world, then we are fulfilling the God inside us.

If we are following the path of spirituality, we have to be one hundred percent faithful to our path. If we have a spiritual Master, we have to be one hundred percent faithful to him. We have to be faithful to our inner life, to the path and to the Master we follow. But a day will come when we will realise that we can be faithful to the inner discipline, the path and the Master only when we are faithful to ourselves.

When we perform any action, we have to feel in this action the life of God. When we are eating, we have to feel that the food is God. If we can see and feel God in everything and feel our constant oneness with God, then automatically we will be faithful to ourselves, and when we are faithful to ourselves, we are bound to get what we are aspiring for.

A seeker of the supreme Truth
Has only one necessity,
And that necessity is
The earth-liberating
And Heaven-manifesting God.

About Sri Chinmoy

Sri Chinmoy is a fully realised spiritual Master dedicated to inspiring and serving those seeking a deeper meaning in life. Through his teaching of meditation, his music, art and writings, his athletics and his own life of dedicated service to humanity, he tries to offer ways of finding inner peace and fulfilment.

Born in Bengal in 1931, Sri Chinmoy entered an ashram (spiritual community) at the age of 12. His life of intense spiritual practice included meditating for up to 14 hours a day, together with writing poetry, essays and devotional songs, doing selfless service and practising athletics. While still in his early teens, he had many profound inner experiences and attained spiritual realisation. He remained in the ashram for 20 years, deepening and expanding his realisation, and in 1964 came to New York City to share his inner wealth with sincere seekers.

Today, Sri Chinmoy serves as a spiritual guide to students in centres around the world. He advocates "the path of the heart" as the simplest way to make rapid spiritual progress. By meditating on the spiritual heart, he teaches, the seeker can discover his own inner treasures of peace, joy, light and love. The role of a spiritual Master, according to Sri Chinmoy, is to instruct his students in the inner life and elevate their consciousness so that these inner riches can illumine their lives. In return he asks his students to meditate regularly and to nurture the inner qualities he helps them bring to the fore.

Sri Chinmoy teaches that love is the most direct way for a seeker to approach the Supreme. When a child feels love for his father, it does not matter how great the father is in the world's eye; through his love the child feels only his oneness with his father and his father's possessions. This same approach, applied to the Supreme, permits the seeker to feel that the Supreme and His own Eternity, Infinity and Immortality are the seeker's own.

This philosophy of love, Sri Chinmoy feels, expresses the deepest bond between man and God, who are aspects of the same unified consciousness. In the life-game, man fulfils himself in the Supreme by realising that God is his own highest Self. The Supreme reveals Himself through man, who serves as His instrument for world-transformation and perfection.

In the traditional Indian fashion, Sri Chinmoy does not charge a fee for his spiritual guidance, nor does he charge for his frequent concerts or public meditations. His only fee, he says, is the seeker's sincere inner cry. He takes a personal interest in each of his students, and when he accepts a student, he takes full responsibility for that individual's inner progress. In New York, Sri Chinmoy meditates in person with his students several times a week and offers a regular Friday evening meditation session for the general public. Students living outside New York see Sri Chinmoy during worldwide gatherings that take place three times a year, during visits to New York or during the Master's frequent trips to their cities. They find that the inner bond between Master and student transcends physical separation. Sri Chinmoy accepts students at all levels of spiritual development, from beginners to advanced seekers, and lovingly guides them inwardly and outwardly according to their individual needs.

Sri Chinmoy personally leads an active life, demonstrating most vividly that spirituality is not an escape from the world, but a means of transforming it. He has written over a thousand books, which include plays, poems, stories, essays, commentaries and answers to questions on spirituality. He has painted thousands of mystical paintings, and his drawings of "soul-birds" number in the millions. He has also composed thousands of devotional songs. Performing his own musical compositions on a wide variety of instruments, he has offered hundreds of Peace Concerts in cities around the world.

A naturally gifted athlete and a firm believer in the spiritual benefits of physical fitness, Sri Chinmoy encourages his students to participate in sports. Under his inspirational guidance, the international Sri Chinmoy Marathon Team organises hundreds of road races, including the longest certified race in the world (3,100 miles), and stages a biennial global relay run for peace. In the field of weightlifting Sri Chinmoy has also achieved phenomenal feats of strength, demonstrating that inner peace gained through meditation can be a tangible source of outer strength.

For more information about Sri Chinmoy, to learn how to become his student, or to attend free meditation classes at a Sri Chinmoy Centre near you, please contact:

Aum Publications
86-10 Parsons Blvd.
Jamaica, NY 11432

OTHER BOOKS BY SRI CHINMOY

Meditation:
Man-Perfection in God-Satisfaction
Presented with the simplicity and clarity that have
become the hallmark of Sri Chinmoy's writings,
this book is easily one of the most comprehensive
guides to meditation available.
Topics include: Proven meditation techniques
that anyone can learn • How to still the restless
mind • Developing the power of concentration •
Carrying peace with you always • Awakening the
heart centre to discover the power of your soul •
The significance of prayer. Plus a special section
in which Sri Chinmoy answers questions on a
wide range of experiences often encountered in
meditation. $9.95

Beyond Within:
A Philosophy for the Inner Life
*"How can I carry on the responsibilities of life and
grow inwardly to find spiritual fulfilment?"*
When your simple yearning to know the purpose
of your life and feel the reality of God has you

swimming against the tide, then the wisdom and guidance of a spiritual Master who has crossed these waters is priceless. Sri Chinmoy offers profound insight into humanity's relationship with God, and sound advice on how to integrate the highest spiritual aspirations into daily life.

Topics include: The spiritual journey • The transformation and perfection of the body • The psyche • Meditation • The relationship between the mind and physical illness • Using the soul's will to conquer life's problems • How you can throw away guilt • Overcoming the fear of failure • The purpose of pain and suffering • Becoming conscious of your own divine nature • and more.

$13.95

My Life's Soul-Journey: Daily Meditations for Ever-Increasing Spiritual Fulfilment

In this volume of daily meditations, Sri Chinmoy offers inspiring thoughts and practical guidelines for those who seek a life of ever-increasing inner fulfilment. In these pages, the simple yet powerful language of the heart rings clear with the message of love, compassion, inner peace and oneness with the world and all its people. Each day's offering resonates with the innate goodness of humanity and encourages the reader to bring this goodness to the fore. $13.95

Death and Reincarnation

This deeply moving book has brought consolation and understanding to countless people faced with the loss of a loved one or fear of their own mortality. Sri Chinmoy explains the secrets of death, the afterlife and reincarnation. $7.95

Yoga and the Spiritual Life

Specifically tailored for Western readers, this book offers rare insight into the philosophy of Yoga and Eastern mysticism. It offers novices as well as advanced seekers a deep understanding of the spiritual side of life. Of particular interest is the section on the soul and the inner life. $8.95

The Summits of God-Life:
Samadhi and Siddhi

A genuine account of the world beyond time and space, this is Sri Chinmoy's firsthand account of states of consciousness that only a handful of Masters have ever experienced. Not a theoretical or philosophical book, but a vivid and detailed description of the farthest possibilities of human consciousness. $6.95

The Three Branches of India's Life-Tree: *Commentaries on the Vedas, the Upanishads and the Bhagavad Gita*

This book brings together in one volume Sri Chinmoy's commentaries on the Vedas, the Upanishads and the Bhagavad Gita, three ancient Indian scriptures which are the foundations of the Hindu spiritual tradition. His approach is clear and practical, and at the same time profound and richly poetic. In a style unmistakably his own, Sri Chinmoy makes direct and personal contact with the reader, who joins him on a journey through the wisdom of these celebrated classics. This book is both an excellent introduction for readers who are coming to the subject for the first time, and a series of illumining meditations for those who already know it well. On the strength of his own inner realisation, Sri Chinmoy enters into these Indian treasurehouses of spirituality and offers their ancient wisdom to the modern spiritual seeker. He is fresh and powerful in expression, but also lyrical and soulful as only a spiritual Master who is also a poet can be.

$13.95

Kundalini: The Mother-Power

En route to his own spiritual realisation, Sri Chinmoy attained mastery over the Kundalini and occult powers. In this book he explains techniques for awakening the Kundalini and the chakras. He warns of the dangers and pitfalls to be avoided, and discusses some of the occult powers that come with the opening of the chakras. $7.95

Inner and Outer Peace
A powerful yet simple approach for establishing peace in your own life and the world.
Sri Chinmoy speaks of the higher truths that energise the quest for world peace, giving contemporary expression to the relationship between our personal search for inner peace and the world's search for outer peace. He reveals truths which lift the peace of the world above purely political and historical considerations, contributing his spiritual understanding to the cause of world peace. $7.95

Eastern Light for the Western Mind
Sri Chinmoy's University Talks
In the summer of 1970, in the midst of the social and political upheavals that were sweeping college campuses, Sri Chinmoy embarked on a university lecture tour offering the message of peace and hope embodied in Eastern philosophy. Speaking

in a state of deep meditation, he filled the audience with a peace and serenity many had never before experienced. They found his words, as a faculty member later put it, to be "living seeds of spirituality." These moments are faithfully captured in this volume of 42 talks. $6.95

A Child's Heart and a Child's Dream
Growing Up with Spiritual Wisdom— A Guide for Parents and Children

Sri Chinmoy offers practical advice on a subject that is not only an idealist's dream but every concerned parent's lifeline: fostering your child's spiritual life, watching him or her grow up with a love of God and a heart of self-giving.

Topics include: Ensuring your child's spiritual growth • Education and spirituality—their meeting ground • Answers to children's questions about God • A simple guide to meditation and a special section of children's stories guaranteed to delight and inspire. $7.95

The Master and the Disciple

What is a Guru? There are running gurus, diet gurus and even stock market gurus. But to those in search of spiritual enlightenment, the Guru is not merely an 'expert'; he is the way to their self-realisation. Sri Chinmoy says in this definitive book on the Guru-disciple relationship: "The most important thing a Guru does for his spiritual children is to make them aware of something vast and infinite within themselves, which is nothing other than God Himself."

Topics include: How to find a Guru • How to tell a real spiritual Master from a false one • How to recognise your own Guru • Making the most spiritual progress while under the guidance of a spiritual Master • What it means when a Guru takes on your karma • Plus a special section of stories and plays illustrating the more subtle aspects of the subject. $7.95

Everest-Aspiration

These inspired talks by one who has reached the pinnacle are invaluable guideposts for others who also want to go upward to the highest, forward to the farthest and inward to the deepest.

Topics include: Dream and Reality • Satisfaction • Imagination • Intuition • Realisation

$9.95

Siddhartha Becomes the Buddha

Who exactly was the Buddha? In ten dramatic scenes, Sri Chinmoy answers this question from the deepest spiritual point of view. The combination of profound insight and simplicity of language makes this book an excellent choice for anyone, young or old, seeking to understand one of the world's most influential spiritual figures.

$6.95

Flute Music for Meditation
While in a state of deep meditation, Sri Chinmoy plays his haunting melodies on the echo flute. Its soothing tones will transport you to the highest realms of inner peace and harmony. Ideal for inspiration in your personal meditations.

Cassette, $9.95   CD, $12.95

The Dance of Light:
Sri Chinmoy Plays the Flute
Forty-seven soft and gentle flute melodies that will carry you directly to the source of joy and beauty: your own aspiring heart. Be prepared to float deep, deep within on waves of music that "come from Heaven itself."   Cassette, $9.95

Inner and Outer Peace
A tapestry of music, poetry and aphorisms on inner and outer peace. Sri Chinmoy's profoundly

227

inspiring messages are woven into a calm and up-lifting musical composition with the Master chanting and playing the flute, harmonium, esraj, cello, harpsichord and synthesizer.

Cassette, $9.95

Ecstasy's Trance:
Esraj Music for Meditation

The esraj, often described as a soothing combination of sitar and violin, is Sri Chinmoy's favourite instrument. With haunting intensity, he seems to draw the music from another dimension. The source of these compositions is the silent realm of the deepest and most sublime meditation. Listen to the music and enter this realm, a threshold rarely crossed in the course of one's lifetime.

Cassette, $9.95

My Prayerful Salutation to the United Nations—*Fifty Peace Concerts*

To honour the United Nations 50th anniversary, Sri Chinmoy performed fifty Peace Concerts around the world. Each disc on this 4 CD set contains 73 minutes of astounding music. Sri Chinmoy plays dozens of instruments including grand piano, kalimba, Viscount synthesizer, echo flute, bamboo flute, xylophone, marimba, esraj and cello.

4 CDs, $29.95

To order books or tapes, request a catalogue, or find out more about Sri Chinmoy or the Sri Chinmoy Centres worldwide, please write to:

AUM PUBLICATIONS
86-10 Parsons Blvd.
Jamaica, NY 11432

When ordering a book or cassette, please send a check or money order made out to Aum Publications. Please send $3.50 postage for the first item and $.50 for each additional item (max. $5.50).